BREAKING THROUGH:
How to Make Your Dreams Come True Against All Odds
By:
Amy Leigh McCorkle

Chapter 1
2011: Ground Zero

To paraphrase one of my favorite acceptance speeches of all time by one of my favorite actors, Russell Crowe, "to anyone living on the downside of advantage, and you are relying purely on courage, it is possible."

And my God, is it ever. To quote the actor, Maurice Benard, whose advocacy got me into treatment, "To everyone who has bipolar disorder, if I can do it so can you".

What's the point of reading forward? Haven't I said everything I've got to say on my life and the fact my brain is wired differently? Strangely enough I feel pulled to share further. If a speak specifically to big dreams and scaling the high mountains, then yes I still have a lot to say.

Every journey of a thousand miles starts with a single step. You've heard the preamble multiple times. But it bears repeating. Over twenty years ago I had a bipolar breakdown. The diagnosis was a relief but going through something so isolating and painful and weird, was hard. Almost from the beginning I wanted, no *needed* to share my story. This first part of my story had many villains both real and imagined.

Like many people, at the beginning of the recovery journey I lost myself to the diagnosis. I allowed myself to be defined by my illness. And for the first six months after being diagnosed, it seemed my writing muse had dried up and left nothing behind to create with.

Though nothing is quite the hell that a dysphoric mania is, not being able to write, when that is your passion, is a special hell all of its own. But there are breakthroughs that happen all along the journey.

Ironically, today, May 5, 2021 is the anniversary of Russell Crowe's Gladiator. In April of 2000 I began to see previews for it. That movie and his iconic performance became the midwife for reclaiming my creative voice.

Granted I wasn't writing great stories, but I was creating again, and when you are a shell of the person you were before a mental breakdown, you thank God and your support network, for any joy or light the darkness. And in 2000 Russell Crowe's gladiator, Maximus stirred something in my imagination and heart and compelled me to write once more.

I told you that to tell you this.

In 2010 I wrote Another Way to Die. Inspired by an entirely different muse. Daniel Craig's James Bond in Casino Royale. The ultimate tragic tale of romance, love, and betrayal.

Where the scenes of Maximus fighting another gladiator and tigers and lit me up for Russell Crowe. It had been the preview for Craig's Bond emerging from the deep blue ocean, his body cut for days in those blue trunks/speedo. In his eyes were a million stories and instantly I fell in creative love and wanted to tell them all.

I wrote the book in May of 2010 and then promptly allowed it to set on my computer's hard drive and collect dust. Why? Fear of success? Fear of failure? Fear of both maybe.

I wish I could say it was a happy circumstance that compelled me to take control of my career. I will say, playing in my own sandbox, watching films and reading books, and worshipping Russell Crowe and Maurice Benard from afar over the years helped me to slowly develop my voice.

So that when Daniel Craig came along and fired my creative soul up, I had no idea what was happening in the grand scheme of things. There are many reasons why the actor has become my hero on many fronts, but we'll get to that later. It was as if I'd fallen down a rabbit hole where my creative hopes and dreams were simmering.

In November of 2010 my best friend's dad was admitted to the hospital for liver transplant surgery, as his stay there was prolonged, and his health declined I began to realize two three things. 1) He probably wasn't coming home. 2)Life was short. Seize the day. 3)As far as my writing and filmmaking dreams were concerned, the mountain wasn't going to come to Mohammed, I was going to have to go to it and scale it myself.

Or to paraphrase Steve Harvey I was going to have to make the first of my many leaps of faith followed by focused, determined action. So what did that mean? That meant take proactive steps.

Fortuitously, friend and fellow author told me about a free online writing conference, digicon, hosted by Savvy Authors.

To any would be authors out there, Savvy Authors, is a resource rich website with classes, workshops, seminars, bootcamps, pitchfests, and conferences year round.

Digicon was one such conference, and Pam insisted I check it out. I signed up. Twilight was huge at the time and I could not understand ADULT WOMEN's fascination with a passive voiced heroine. I didn't find the movies any better. But let's face it, Stephanie Meyer tapped a vein and hit a nerve. Any woman's success is proof it can be done.

I pitched 4 publishers and 1 agent with Another Way to Die. Got accepted by all of them. Refused the agent (hey even smart girls make dumb decisions), but smartly accepted MuseItUp's offer of publication where they would groom me into a much better writer and prepare me for things to come.

That was in February of 2011.

I wrote No Ordinary Love in April of 2011. Received my second publication contract with Muse. In November I penned my futuristic romance, GLADIATOR: The Gladiator Chronicles. Signed my third contract with Muse in December of the same year.

At the time it felt like a major BOOM. And for me it was. It would mark my first success in the legitimate publishing would. These booms and mini booms would come to be the hallmark of my career. Writing non-stop, arduous climbing, and rejection, followed by a mini boom or BOOM!

The breakthroughs make the journey worth it. And January 2011 was the first BOOM! I experienced. Thank you Savvy Authors. Thank you MuseITUp and thank you Pam, for your support and friendship over the years.

First lesson, submit your work. It's the only way you'll ever move forward.

Chapter 2
Sweatfest: The Local Journey Begins

What is Sweatfest, you may ask? In 2011 I attended my first convention. It was the single most miserable physical experience I had at a convention. But I met an individual who welcomed me into the local writing community with open arms. Stephen Zimmer was the kind of writer and filmmaker who also mentored countless writers, along with his own creative pursuits.

In 2011 the only reason I knew about Stephen, was because of Pam, and an actor I had worked with, James Tackett. And there was this little thing called Fandom Fest taking place at the Fern Valley Convention Center.

I reached out to Stephen on Facebook and he got me on some panels, most memorably with Maurice Broaddus who I would become friends with. Slight detour, I was on Twitter one morning and Maurice was talking about how nervous he was at the possibility of being diagnosed with bipolar disorder. I tweeted back, it was going to be okay and that medication and therapy had helped me a lot. He said good, if this doesn't work then I'm blaming you.

We shared a conspiratorial laugh. And at the first Imaginarium we exchanged books and took a photo together.

As it was at that first Fandom Fest I attended I had vendor table. And as it happened the air conditioner was freaking fritz. The organizers shoved all the vendors in the center of the Fern Valley Conference Center where the pool was. It had the effect of turning the entire building into a steam bath.

I knew no one. My tablemate would become a friend, then someone who would c=go on to savage me. You live. You learn. She was a poison. No need to name names. She was toxic. But what I've come to learn is that toxic individuals are the biggest burden to themselves, and are just in a lot of pain.

At the time I weighed well over three hundred pounds. My blood sugar was out of control. And all I had at the vendor table were bookmarks, romance trading cards, and a legal pad trying to start a mailing list.

I got so heat sick my meds started acting up. I had double vision and was nauseous. I wasn't about to stay. But on the last day, an author was handing out the signed copy of her book. There Stephen was, handing out the book and wishing me well.

My ebooks had yet to be published. The one due out in October of 2011, No Ordinary Love, had been inspired by Cowboys and Aliens. As much as Maurice Benard got me into treatment through his openness about his own recovery journey, and Russell had reawakened my storytelling heart.

Daniel Craig and his work would become my creative muse.

He *looked like* my heroes. His acting style suited my writing and my imagination. And those eyes of his could convey any number of things. I like to say when I write manuscript length prose I get to fall in love for 50-100k words at time.

When I write scripts it's about empowerment and love. And whether I called it by name or not, the illnesses I lived with everyday, bipolar disorder, anxiety, and PTSD, found their way into my stories.

In 2011, my advocacy work, and my most powerful movie to date, Letters to Daniel wasn't even a twinkle in my eye. I was just an author, seeking success and desperate for all my dreams to come true, really like any aspiring author.

It was clear Sweatfest was not the place where all my dreams would come true, but because Stephen was there championing *all* of the authors, I came back in 2012 and even submitted scripts in 2013 and 2014, winning in 2013 with the adaptation of Bounty Hunter from my bestselling novel of the same name.

Sweatfest eventually peaked in 2013 and then hit a slow decline until 2017 when most of their guests cancelled, the bottom fell out of their film festival, and it died an ignominious death in an abandoned Macy's in it's final year.

On the other end, Stephen Zimmer went on to found Imaginarium in 2014. There was something sweet and special about that first year. But on to that in future chapters.

In 2011 I was a social awkward, fat, insecure nerd. At Sweatfest, Organizers notwithstanding, I had found my tribe. Authors and filmmakers.

All that playing in the sandbox had given me three books and a nurturing way to develop my storytelling and truth telling voices. Which would eventually become the same thing.

I survived the brutal heat. Overbearing panelists, well meaning naysayers, and bonded with APEX Publishing's Maurice Broaddus, fellow Blackwrym alum L. Andrew Cooper and his husband as he says, is his Missy in terms of bipolar disorder and caregiving.

Fandom Fest 2011 was important even if it wasn't the most smoothly run convention. It proved to me there were other oddballs like myself out there swimming and thrashing about trying to break in.

What I quickly learned well, over my recovery is that gratitude for every step of success is essential.

In 2012 I through a book launch. My three cousins cosplayed GLADIATOR my book, and two mysterious gentlemen. One of them my parents age and balding with glasses, and the other was his son.

When I opened the floor for questions he said his name was Lee Mont and that he had come specifically to see me. He said his last name was McCorkle. Turns out he was my biological father's first cousin.

So even though Fandom Fest nearly killed me physically (in their defense I was 60 pounds heavier), it gave me a relative to love on my father's side. And connected me to some amazing authors and Stephen.

I was so inspired by the first Imaginarium, I made a documentary about it. But more on that later.

At Fandom Fest I sold lots of books and made lots of disgruntled author friends. Understandably so.

So I guess my second piece of advice is, be grateful for every success, no matter how small. Because you can rewire your entire thought process with it. I'm not talking take your pill and do therapy and everything will be rosy. There's some real shitty stuff that comes with bipolar disorder. Paralyzing numbness, dysphoric mania, deadening depression and crazy levels of anxiety.

Medicine, therapy and a support network are crucial, but what I'm talking about in the chapter is essential, and I resisted doing it for years. Until inspired by Missy and my publisher at the time of all people, to start a blog. And that's how Letters to Daniel came to be.

Chapter 3
The Birth of Letters to Daniel

Letters to Daniel was the child of conversations with my publisher, my best friend, and of course my discovery of Daniel Craig in Casino Royale. A blog. My therapist kept saying you need to journal Amy. And yet I resisted at every turn.

Then finally in May 2013 all of these element had simmered, stewed, and blended long enough that one day I thought, hey I'll write an open letter to my favorite actor, Daniel Craig. I was about halfway through the letter when I realized I was trying to cram every single life experience in one blog post. Which on the face it was ridiculous.

When I realized the reality was he would never see the blog something shifted inside of me. I was finally ready to tell my story. And God/Universe was presenting me with a way to share my story with others, and not be so self-conscious about it.

Daniel became this invisible, non-judgmental audience who I could spill my guts to and unburden myself to. At the same to I got the biggest response audience-wise for my work. Which for me wasn't work. I was simply telling my life story.

Every morning I would wake and write the days emotions and navigate them. Along with some raw and gritty memories from the past. Everyday it felt like I had taken a shower and scrubbed my past faults and wounds away. Not that I was perfect. Not that I am perfect, far from it. By journaling with these letters I was healing, growing stronger, and refusing to be defined by my illness.

I was rediscovering my power and finding my voice.

My career seem to do a steady climb up at the time. Was it what some call success? I was writing and publishing fiction on a regular basis. Never had I mastered non-fiction. So I collected the letters up to that point and put them in a book.

With help from Lea Schizas and Delilah K. Stephans I was able to self-publish the first volume of letters in October of 2013. This became my first non-fiction bestseller.

There was something about this book that opened up a dialogue at book signings and conventions. People opened up about their own pain, or the fact they knew someone with bipolar disorder.

Letters to Daniel became the engine to my writing career while I grew stronger and stronger. There would be a second volume and a revised third edition which would contain two thirds new material and go on to be a bestseller in seven different countries and a finalist in the EPIC competition in the non-fiction category.

So, back up a few steps.

At this point I had eleven Amazon Bestsellers. Spearheaded by an unexpected success of me sharing my life story. This was 2016.

In the late winter/early spring of 2014 Stephen Zimmer announced the creation of Imaginarium, a creative writing convention, that was going to have a small film festival component. I asked if it was going to have a documentary category. To which Stephen said you can have a premiere and a Q&A for it.

Folks, the only thing I had was a title. I created a 345 dollar budgeted documentary. I collected twelve of the letters that packed the most punch, gathered as many photos of me as possible, and given that I could get no local help as I wasn't on anyone's radar, and I had not travelled to other festivals, I was my own narrator. As far as local help it was Pam and Missy coming to the rescue.

I edited the film on Pam's PC with Vegas software. Missy purchased the more expensive things. And then there were the submission fees for six festivals. It was only ever intended for the film to be screened and seen at the 2014 Imaginarium. It was a fluke that I submitted to the Indie Gathering in May of the same year, where it won it's first award, before it actually screened at Imaginarium where it would win its second award.

I was sticking my toe into the oceanic waters of mental health advocacy. Sure it feels like everyone is doing it now, but I truly believe that there is enough room for all of us, because it needs all of us.

But even as Letters the blog continues to this day, it had to start somewhere with the faith of a mustard seed. Dealing with my bipolar disorder is a full time job, but Letters to Daniel would go on in 2015 to be penned as a narrative script that Missy and I partnered up on. (Here's a secret, Missy and I co-write every script.) She produced Letters to Daniel so that I could direct it in 2019.

In the HIGFA towards the end of the year I won Best Director and the film also took home the Outstanding Editing.

Then to prove God has a nasty sense of humor, covid shut down everything. And the tour took place online.

But before we move ahead the actual filming of Letters to Daniel was amazing. With genius Mark Maness as my DP. Missy as the JOAT (Jill of All Trades). Me as director with an amazing cast in place full gifted local talented. I filmed it all for 6k.

Are there flaws? Sure there are. But as an executive said, you made a good film for six thousand dollars.

But the reality is, I would have never gotten to wear it would go next if not for another festival and the opportunities they offered.

The truth is from first published novel to this moment has taken ten years. And if you count the years spent working to get stable, finding my voice, and reclaiming my power then make it twenty plus years.

The birth of Letters to Daniel has really been a journey, and it's one I've been on with my creative partner for some time. As the sweet outweighs the bitter finally in my career I have to tell you not all festivals are created equal.

Even the ones you love will shift around on you. So far you've heard me mention three festivals. I will add another. Turn the page to find out how they all made a difference in my life.

Chapter 4

1 Convention, 1 Film Festival, & A Preamble to A Career

They say things have a beginning middle and end. My life has been full seasons where I thought, yup, yup, this is it. Everyone who ever doubted me is going to rue the day they ever did. And then, another creation comes along, and another festival, and finally another project.

I don't think instant success at a young age helps prepare you for anything. Especially in Hollywood. You see where even the brightest and best can be chewed up and spit out by the limachine.

Even though I am, as of this writing forty-five years old, I am glad I was not successful in Hollywood in my twenties. As some may know it took ten years to find my voice due to the illness and perhaps ten more to refine it to the point I could tell you how I did it.

Let me preface this with, no one reaches the top (and I'm certainly not the top, just standing on the verge of mainstream success), or gets to where they're going the same way as anyone else. This is how I've done it. That doesn't mean you have to do it that way.

The one thing I do though, is hustle every day. Grind constantly. Writing grounds me and sets me stable like nothing else. Coupled with my medications, therapy and the care I receive from those who love and fight for me, sustain me in the harder times, and makes writing a pure pleasure.

So where do I start, probably with Imaginarium. It's local, a wonderful and regional convention addressing the arts, while specializing in the writing prism. Even in the film festival that is attached yearly.

Imaginarium was born in 2014. I had several books and even managed to make some money. Let's see if I can remember all of them. Gemini's War, Gemini's Legacy, Letters to Daniel Vol 1 & 2, Blackout, the Gladiator Chronicles. And my proof of concept documentary, Letters to Daniel premiered at the first Imaginarium.

What Imaginarium and Letters had in common, was that for their perspective creators it was the beginning for their visions. Stephen was stepping out on faith for me and by placing my art with his festival and sponsoring them initially I was saying I believe in your vision.

I'm not a regular sponsor anymore, mostly because my money has gone elsewhere to build my career. But early on I was thrilled to support them. They supported me. They supported my work.

Did that mean I won all the time? No. In fact they lean towards scifi/horror/fantasy in their tastes. That's not really sleight. They have been welcoming every year and I always have some take away from it.

Imaginarium was the first place where I could build a network of colleagues meaning authors. There is an intimacy to Imaginarium that brings friends together and indie and self publishing professionals together. Small presses also join in.

That's where I gleaned the most benefit from Imaginarium. The support early on in my career really served to build a solid foundation on which everything else was to come.

What I recommend is if you're starting out you find the convention or film festival that can serve as that for you. If you live in the Midwest of Southeastern part of the United States the web address is entertheimaginarium.com. It used to happen in the late summer or the fall, it has now moved to the mid-summer in July. It features online and in-person portions. They are attempting to spread their wings. I will always love Imaginarium for the role it played in Letters to Daniel early film development. I don't know where I would have gone with it initially otherwise.

Even though I won at Fandom Fest's screenwriting competition. And Imaginarium was my first screening of Letters to Daniel the documentary, I'll always consider the Indie Gathering the first traditional film festival that me and Missy to breakthrough at. And it was a total fluke that I had found them.

Before the demise of Withoutabox (a submission platform) they would send out upcoming deadlines to other festivals. In May of 2014 the Indie Gathering came to my attention.

I have to be honest I've been to my share of comic cons, signings, and festivals and they are not created equal. Some are shady, some are a money grab, and then you find those gems that are meant to nurture you along your way to your greatness or on your path to you all that you've ever wanted.

Where as Imaginarium gave me that early support, Indie Gathering gave access to the ability to network with the Ohio and somewhat international flavored communities of directors, writers, composers, fx artists, and stunt people.

Ray is a salt of the earth guy, and the founder of Indie Gathering and Kristina is a fabulous festival director who can rattle off several hundred script projects and who they belong to.

Speaking of someone who runs her own festival now I am amazed at this. We won 5 awards that first year. Four screenwriting awards and one for Letters to Daniel the proof of concept documentary.

There I would meet Brandon X Bell, Doug Kaufman, Valyo Gennoff. Through them, Maria Christian, Abigail Yates, Vanessa Card, and John Spalding, people who would hail from all over to eventually help make Letters to Daniel a reality.

They would put us on the map and help make over twenty films including Letters to Daniel: The Motion Picture in 2019. They nurtured my talent and recognized me and Missy's work until we were ready for the above.

He would take the straw that would stir the drink and put the final elements together.

Let me say, if you are hardcore serious about making it in the Arts. And by that I mean survive it's sleights, cycles, ups, downs and triumphs, you won't be ready for the next step until you've gotten your start, been nurtured, and taken the bold move of declaring your dreams already a reality.

Now if your ready to hear about the game changer turn the page.

Chapter 5
AOF MEGAFEST

Tell the truth, some festivals lay the foundation, some act as midwife for certain stages of your career. And others take you to another level completely. Now let me take a moment to say my way is not the only way.

I did not go to film school.

I do not have a college degree.

I do not live in Los Angeles.

I do not live in Atlanta.

I do not live in New York City.

Name a film city (Austin, or anywhere in Florida).

I heard Geeta Patel tell her story. She didn't go to film school either. That she made films that looked like crap before, "making it". About people's perceptions that there wasn't a need for her kinds of stories tell.

Today I also identified with Janet Mock, to some degree. Being an invisible segment of society (I have bipolar disorder, anxiety and PTSD), yet I walk through world with white privilege and cis straight woman. Janet Mock is a beast and a beautiful black woman period. And has so much talent and education. God bless her.

If I can inspire the next generation or my generation or the generation who came before me to follow their bliss (which I know sounds hopelessly hokey) but it's true. I heard Geeta Patel put it this way, I knew I had made it, when I got to make what I wanted to make.

I'm having that moment.

Twenty plus years of writing, healing, and recovery and half of that with a careful cultivation and hard work which has lead to that moment.

Actually executing Letters to Daniel was the start of that. I started my active filmmaking career in 2014. In 2016 I was coming off some bad experiences, where I didn't believe people when they told me who they really were. It really screwed with my head. And it made me very paranoid.

But executing Letters to Daniel, wouldn't happen until 2019.

Betrayals and paranoia ruled the first half of 2016. People promising the world. Lying about it. Predatory people telling me I shouldn't be a writer or a filmmaker. Encountering well meaning but toxic people saying I would never get Letters to Daniel made if I insisted on directing.

Then I stumbled onto AOF Megafest and along with it the AOF familia, Del and Theresa Weston. My gut told me put the effort into going to their festival. Not just because it was in California, but because there was something whispering in my ear that this was where things were going change. But I would have to take that leap of faith.

Let me say, I've been to some festivals. And AOF is and always will be first in my heart. They embraced me, Missy and our work. They took a big chance on us where others wanted to use us to their end, AOF offered a free market of opportunities. A street that went both ways. They saw something in us that perhaps we did not see in ourselves. I wanted to be a working screenwriter and director. Del said you are. Theresa said we believe in you. That first year the love was so overwhelming. So healing.

Let me repeat that, so healing.

That was life changing.

Being at a large festival, but it still have that intimate feeling was so heady. Even when I had an anxiety attack and broke down. They took care of me. It's not the awards me and Missy won, but the nominations that made us feel like we were amongst our peers AND THEY RESPECTED us.

Winning Best New Writer and two awards for our documentary, Letters to Daniel, was so overwhelming. I met many people several of them became mentors and friends. And eventually out of that group, their were collaborators, and from that I've added Del, Anabelle Munro and Lureen Wu to my core group as such we've become a team, along with the already brilliant Missy.

I've learned a significant lesson over the years. And it was crystalized into for me in a way that I can pass it on to you. "Making it" isn't a destination. It's an emotion. A realization. That you are blessed to be doing what you love. Whether you need a side hustle to support that bliss or you are able to do it full time everyone needs help getting there.

AOF, Del and Theresa are the reason Missy I have "made it". How you've made it? How did I know? The day we did the martini shot on the last day of filming of Letters to Daniel was when this feeling started.

The breakthrough moment of success, where I felt like I was coming into my own. At the end of a 3 hour long dinner with Joshua Carpenter of Green Apple Entertainment where he said yes to the The Guardian's Sacrifice, as a limited 5 episode series. And a morning pitch of Gemini's Rising aka The Assassin's Redemption after he said we're going to help you make this and when it's ready distribute it. Yes, indeed that glow of you're stepping into your dream and embracing it, washed over me. And the truth is, I would have never been able to get past some pretty hurtful betrayals if it was not for the showering of unconditional love and faith that they had for me.

AOF was a life changer for me. They picked me up off the ground, set me on my feet again and become the wind at my back.

When I won at AOF in 2016 and screened at the glorious Krikorian Theater. Where I experienced my film onscreen for the first time. Not just a projector and a screen in a hotel room (although any chance you get a chance to screen your film is an honor), but there is a difference.

AOF was a profound, life changing experience. They provided a free market of opportunities, and unending source of unconditional love.

They understand where someone like me is coming from. Meaning someone with serious mental illness stretching herself beyond her limitations, but at times being forced to recognize and manage that illness.

I knew AOF was home when I experienced an a full blown anxiety attack and the festival director herself took care of me. Let me say I love Theresa Weston. She and Del are the reason I was able to grow as a filmmaker. AOF acted as this kind of incubator for knocked around creatives.

They believed in me even when I doubted myself. They were the yes I was searching for. As I grew and learned and capitalized on the opportunities given and *learned* through them it was okay to be ambitious. It was okay to desire recognition. It was okay to want that Oscar. Winning that first year altered everything.

Winning didn't matter as much anymore. I'd loved the work before. Now I was driven to create, my mission as a mental health advocate came into sharp relief, and I continued to hustle. To quote Hamilton I was, and continue to be Non-Stop.

Chapter 6
Maurice Benard: The Reason I Got Into Treatment

In October of 1999 it had become clear something was very wrong with me. I couldn't function. The house was a disaster area. Simple hygiene was complicated, (I still wrestle with this one). I would cry for hours on end. I couldn't stand the silence. I couldn't stand the sound of someone talking to me. My thoughts raced. My skin crawled. I experienced sleep deprivation on a level I had not experienced heretofor.

Everybody has their heroes and I'm no different. What started out as a mission to create an amazing role for Maurice Benard turned into something else. I wrote constantly, obsessively sending letters. In an intense repetitive way that screamed notice me, take me seriously, I'm borderline in love with your character Sonny Corinthos.

Honestly, it had to be disturbing to some degree. I was in the grips of illness and to say I wasn't myself was an understatement. I was crying through the night. I was only writing letters (which ironically, would put me on the map), and the script I wrote with Missy, well let's just say hers and my craft has improved dramatically in twenty some odd years.

The thing about this is either Maurice has mercifully forgotten about me and those crazy letters, or he does remember, but because he too has bipolar, he understands. Which for me is an incredible blessing, because I adore him as an advocate and I am a big fan of General Hospital and the Ghost & the Whale.

Our careers have this strange parallel thing going. Of course his platform is somewhat bigger than mine at this time. But I don't think it will always be so.

You think that cocky of me to say? Maybe it is. Women in general are punished for showing confidence. We live in a patriarchal society.

I'm not hating on men. I love men. But certain things are ingrained in society as whole. Maurice has made it okay for men to speak about their mental health in an open and healthy way.

His platform? He's Sonny. He's a tv and movie star. And whoever ghost wrote his book did an incredible job of getting him to talk very openly. His story is moving and inspirational. And it has saved many lives. Including mine.

When talking about the industry he says there is little respect for soaps and what they do. Yet the actors in the industry admire them greatly. Every piece of a soap writing machine, especially daytime had me wanting to write for them.

As a child I watched General Hospital with my Aunt Debbie and my Mamaw. My Mamaw, when she was alive, referred to Maurice has her boyfriend. My Aunt Debbie was the victim of covid-19. Yet her love of the ABC soaps lives on in me.

I still love both women fiercely.

Maurice was the first advocate that I could really relate to. That's not to minimize Patty Duke's contributions to the world, I just couldn't relate. She wasn't a contemporary, but that being said, she was amazing. And what she did for those with bipolar disorder was brilliant.

Maurice was an advocate. He would be someone who lit the way very early on.

When I was initially diagnosed it was very hard to find my way. To be twenty-four, full of piss and vinegar, only to be waylaid by an illness which was the Loki of the mental illnesses. Charming and sly, glowing and brilliant one minute, raging and violent the next, sobbing and inconsolable the another, bipolar disorder, can and will at times make you it's bitch.

That doesn't mean you can't have the life you wanted. Maurice taught me that, it just means you have to heal, and surrender to the process of recovery. Recovery is not an endpoint. Not in any real sense.

And in the beginning, success, as I had envisioned it fell away and slipped through my fingers. I had to realize that first came the hard work of recovery and healing. I wanted share my story straight off the bat.

I had always felt a kinship with Maurice. The diagnosis made me realize why, when I didn't know the man, I felt such a connection to him. I stumbled upon interviews with him where he spoke so openly and honestly about his battle (and getting stable is a battle) and journey in staying stable, that I found a clearer way to go forward in my healing.

What Maurice has managed to accomplish a lot during his recovery, including winning two daytime Emmys, write (someone ghost wrote that I'm sure) a book, and advocate in a way that has led to less stigma and more people seeking help.

I've had the privilege of meeting Maurice either through phone calls, zoom calls, or fan appearances over the last twenty plus years. Each time was an extraordinary experience. Especially the last time as we talked about our professional journeys. As he said, you're me.

I have written memoirs.

I have a podcast.

I write scripts.

I direct movies.

And I advocate for the mentally ill. For me the only thing missing is the adoring wife and four beautiful children at various stages of life.

Truthfully I've never wanted kids. But bring on the furbabies.

Folks Maurice will forever be my first creative love. And my favorite mickey mouse mobster.

Maurice was the reason I got into treatment, and as my first muse, I wrote a gazillion stories with him. A relaxing way to learn my craft without the stress. Maurice was a really big part of that, and while he is no longer a muse he, along with Missy, and information from my sister Sara led me into treatment and ultimately to the beginning of this journey.

The Universe is a beautiful thing. God is a loving God. Because of both I am blessed to be where I am at. Maybe your muse isn't a soap opera star, but someone or something else is. Whoever it is, whatever your favorite tool in the toolbox is. Keep moving forward with one step in front of the other.

Without Maurice, I might have never known about my illness. Without getting into treatment I wouldn't be where I am now, living the dream.

Chapter 7
What Does Success Mean to You?

I've been reflecting on what does it mean to have "made it", ever since I heard Geela Patel say what it was for her. Before I unpack that I have to unpack some of the bitterness and joy I have experienced along the way. And I hope it helps you along in your journey.

Here me when I say this. There will be obstacles. Walls to climb. And setbacks. You will experience adversity in this journey. Success will sneak up on you in increments. You will crawl, stumble, leap, crash, and if you work insanely hard with passion for what you do, and prove persistence is the most important quality, you will soar. In other words my anthems were originally I Will Survive and Independent Women. I rocked the songs before I rocked the reality.

Success is in the eye of the beholder.

Seems like such a simple concept, right? Yet not everyone gets. Success is bliss, is joy, is wellness and healing. It is a process, much like recovery, it is not an endpoint. Because it is ongoing.

And like all good things, you don't get there alone. Especially if you are a survivor of sex abuse, and live with bipolar disorder everyday. You survive this adversity, you will find joy. And you will either find your muse, or they will definitely find you. And you will definitely find and reclaim what is a powerful voice.

Have I made it?

The question demands to be broken down a couple of different ways.

To see me now means you see the end result over twenty years of work on my career and my person.

The professional stakes were and are high for what I do.

So when faced with the people who don't believe, and there will be, I know it will be hard for it not to matter. If you are woman it will be hard not to notice places where it is a sausagefest.

What do I mean by that?

I don't mean being surrounded by men who are creative, I mean being at a festival when the men and the work they do they are coveted and slobbered all over. While your work is there also, you feel like a simple check.

Perhaps early on in the festival you won a trinket or two. Then you're singled out as, "not as legit as the others".

I know what that's like.

It burns.

It sucks.

And it made me mad as hell.

I was just as decorated as freaking sci-fi fantasy storyteller as the ones at an insignificant convention as the so called "more successful" ones were.

It made me bitter for a time. And then I realized I didn't need all that angst. What was the answer? Spew my venom at these people? Scream until my voice was raw? Demand that they honor me?

It was hard not to get a complex when they changed the definition of an award twice in an effort to avoid giving it to me as a sponsor. And indeed I did get a complex. Then it happened recognition at other places for my talent. Respect whereas at this place it was sorely lacking. Love for me and my work, whereas this place saw me as a check.

AOF Megafest has consistently awarded me and mentored me over the last six years, and it has been during this time my skills have undergone a transformation. That I have met the people who have changed my life.

I guess one of those times I felt I had reached another level in my career for the first time was at that first AOF Megafest.

And what I mean by what does success mean to you, is that you have to make a mental shift as to what success looks like to you.

For the longest time I only saw success as NY traditionally published. Or me standing on the Oscar stage. While I still haven't climbed those particular mountains here are somethings I have accomplished.

I have survived childhood sex abuse.

Even though bipolar has at times made me it's bitch, I have managed to learn to ride the waves of the illness.

This doesn't mean I don't feel pain nor am I anguish free. It just means I have an awareness level with my illness that allows me to function at a level most of the time where it appears as if nothing is wrong. Trust me for those of you who don't have bipolar disorder and don't know how monumental that is, trust me it is HUGE.

I am a published, bestselling, award winning author. Although it is in the small press here are my numbers:

29 published books

Multiple awards for said books

11 Amazon Bestselllers

34 written manuscripts

3 short stories

I am also an award winning co-writer. Me and Melissa have written 39 scripts, of which 37 are award winning.

We have produced/directed 23 films.

Across our body of work we have won a total 134 awards and 70+ nominations.

I am not saying this brag and letting you know that mental illness is no death sentence. And that you don't have to be defined by it.

The first time I felt like I executed everything right was for my film Letters to Daniel. I had to release it to the festival circuit during the year of Covid-19. The run continues today. So far there are 34 wins and 60+ nominations.

I guess the next question is, when do you quantify that you've made it?

The moment for me was at Branson International Film Festival.

I pitched the executive from Green Apple Entertainment distribution for Letters to Daniel. He said yes. Then I pitched my project The Guardian: Sacrifice. He said yes. I pitched Gemini Rising which has since become the Assassin's Redemption, he guaranteed the distribution of it. With stars like TC Stallings, Kevin Sorbo, Tim Culbertson, and my producing partner bringing on the likes (possibly) of Michael Gier and Michael Madsen I feel like the last three or four months have been a whirlwind.

Indeed I feel like my career is skyrocketing. See what I mean, mental illness does not define me, it is a double edged sword that gives and takes.

How did I heal? How was I able to do this?

Therapy, meds, the support of amazing caregivers, and having movies, music, books, plays, and, just the arts in general, to support me.

There was a time when I was so sick the muse left me. But things like General Hospital, The Insider, Gladiator, and A Beautiful Mind kept me writing alone without someone telling me I was doing it wrong.

It was like I was free to play in the sandbox and develop my voice and heal at the same time. Writing what I wanted when I wanted. Even that was a success to be celebrated.

The truth is, you have to realize that in order to realize the big recognizable successes, you have to see it in all the small and medium sized successes. And stop with the excuses.

I don't have time.

Everyone has the same twenty-fours in a day and the same seven days a week.

I have no money.

Go to the library and use their computers. With Covid restrictions loosening that's not a good enough reason anymore.

I have no film equipment.

Go to some local film festivals for godssakes and network with people who do.

No one respects or acknowledges me.

For fucks sake write a script, spread your wings and travel out of state to other festivals and network.

I want to be plucked from obscurity and be discovered ala Lana Turner at the soda shop. To be fair it's easy to want this. But the entertainment and publishing industries are NOT EASY.

I realized, the mountain doesn't come to you. You have to go to the mountain.

You'd think women delude themselves with this fantasy. But I know more grown men wishing for that magical moment. Or really telling me what I did can't possibly work for them. And that they want to be magically discovered.

The thing I can tolerate the least is when people like me say they have similar issues or other obstacles which keep them from succeeding. This pisses me off to no end.

Granted it is harder for us, both because of what we deal with the illness or disability, and conversely because of the way society is set up to view us. But for the love of God don't you dare tell me it's impossible or that you can't. Because that is complete and utter garbage. In other words I call bullshit.

In today's day and age and really at any time your first champion has to be you. Because no one is going to believe in you unless you do. No one will invest in you unless you do. And sometimes those you love most, when the time comes, will do things that sabatoge a maybe mutually held dream. It will force you to make hard choices. Unpopular choices.

How much do you want that dream of Hollywood? The reality is not everybody can deal with what it takes to be in the industry. I have grinded and grinded to reach where I am and there are still stumbling blocks.

My biggest ally is getting cold feet at just wrong time. I don't want to leave her behind because she's been integral up until this point to the journey.

I know what it is, she's afraid of losing her family again because when we first endeavored to dream an impossible dream they punished her harshly for it. She then had the added bonus of dealing with me having a nervous breakdown.

I know she hesitates because family is very important to her. My family is important to me too. But I've lived with my dream for a lifetime. As much as I want to fall in love, I want to be able to do what I love when I want and how I want.

Missy doesn't dream as big as me. And she doesn't do the work to make it happen like I do. Don't get me wrong. Every river has got to have her rock and for over twenty years, Missy has provided me with the structure that has allowed me to build my dream. So in essence, she's in the shadows, while I have sunlight on my face.

I'm not giving up on her though. She will come around and we will move to Las Vegas for the new chapter opening up in our lives. Just like I got her to come around to writing Letters to Daniel. And you all know how that turned out.

What are your blocks? Why are you telling yourself I can't?

Granted, there are times when life calls on you to wait, and the timing is not the best. But look in a mirror and get really honest with yourself. And make a decision. Embrace your destiny, and like Debbie Thomas said, "Just do it."

Chapter 8
It's Gratitude, Gratitude, Gratitude

I'm a competitive person. So much so, that it could destroy the bliss of what I do. In my adolescence I competed in everything imaginable. Chess, debate, field hockey, local and state competitions in music. Except for field hockey I was often the girl, and was always in the position of "proving" myself to the guys.

I was also obsessed with winning.

What's wrong with winning. Nothing really. But when it is the only thing that drives you it can be toxic. There must be the fundamental fact that joy and gratitude bring you.

I've been writing since I was five years old. Reading since that age. Adoring stories pretty much all of my cognizant life. Stories were an escape when life was to hard to deal with. So today is about using gratitude as a way to rewire your brain and heal.

Gratitude is funny thing. Some people, in fact, the more they have of success sometimes the capacity for gratitude strangely goes down. My Dad calls it the bell curve of gratitude. The more that one does for them, the more bitter, self entitled, they become.

Gratitude though, can heal you and help rewire your entire brain. If you let it, if you want it, if you do the work, no matter where you're at in your career or life gratitude can make things change. It takes work. Daily application. And discipline.

It's the simplest thing in the world to do, to be grateful. But it is not always the easiest. People are human. People get mad. And when you are on a movie set things are organized chaos. It is marching an army in a joyous kind of hell. And you have to be kind of crazy to do it over and over again.

Gratitude, at least for me, was quite the game changer.

Gratitude, for me was about finding the joy in the little things. Small victories deserve to be celebrated just as much as the big ones. To mark the milestones with joy and pride in ones writing career are important. You have to find your why. And believe me my why has never been about getting rich and famous. Fame seems chew people up and spit them out.

I write primarily because it feels good and brings me joy. I have fun doing it. And when I'm not writing it's usually a sign that there's something wrong.

One thing I did was change my perspective on what a successful career in the publishing industry was. I was initially electronically published by the epublisher, MuseItUP. Recently, they folded. But they were the first publishing house to take a chance on me. That was ten years ago.

When success came I envisioned it as a NYT bestseller at a big NY traditional publishing house. When I started have success with small presses and self-publishing I had to adjust what that meant for my career.

When I thought of success I thought of a literary agent.

I have been burned by three agents.

That being said everyone has their nightmare stories. And even though those people burned me, I don't think there's evil in them. They are just messed up individuals. And they came into my life as a lesson.

Same as film. You usually see success as mainstream Hollywood movies. But as with the golden age of publishing now there are a ton streamers springing up looking for content. I made my first award winning film in 2014.

Again the dream is the Academy Awards, the Emmys, the Daytime Emmys, and Indie Series Awards. I've had a film's music (Valyo Genoff & Stephanie Ray) longlisted at the Oscars. And been invited to submit to the ISAs.

Lord knows I have gratitude for all that I have achieved.

What I am most grateful is my sanity and stability. Those are hard won. The battle for them was fierce. A little over two years after receiving my first publishing contracts, I created the Letters to Daniel blog. It was a place for me to share my memoirs. It was a place to vent. A place to give thanks. A place to be grateful and express gratitude.

It was raw, gritty, and uncut. It was filled with emotion, I could be irrational at the beginning with indignant rage or self-pity at the start of the letters and by the end a weight would be lifted and I could express compassion, gratitude or both.

I wrote these letters to my favorite actor Daniel Craig. By this time I'm half in love with him as a pretend friend, rather the image I have of him after spilling such raw and intimate things about my journey to stability where my bipolar disorder was concerned.

Gratitude for all of my life experiences. Even the ones which were lessons that hurt. And believe me, they hurt. Lessons which knock you to the ground, leaving you winded, bruised and cut up emotionally, are testing you. Can you get back up?

A writer friend of mine once said, after an especially bruising moment in which I had been left devastated had me flat on my back, don't they know you get back up?

That made me laugh, and it made me feel better. I have gratitude for the lesson, that now setbacks are a moment before the amazing victories that are about to happen, and I really need to hang on to my boots.

Gratitude is also about the daily discipline of applying gratitude to all those emotional cuts and bruises. And getting back up when some asshole knocks us back down for another lesson or two.

My blog was a comforting way to tell my story.

I suppose there is no better way to teach gratitude than to give a place to write about what your grateful for.

In your own words and just to start, what are the five greatest lessons in your life that you have learned? And what is it you have gratitude for most in your life? And what can you do in order to show others the disciplinary nature of the gratitude?

Before moving on answer those questions in your journal.

Chapter 9
What Is Your Why?

My why is I want to get better.

Get better at what?

More like get better at maintaining stability by applying my skills at writing and directing. My craft was the final stepping stone to wellness. And strangely enough, the key to my success, which I am currently enjoying.

For the most part.

Learning to manage my stress levels and maintain emotional balance is an ever evolving journey. The truth is I have no idea which side of the bipolar bed I'm going to wake up on. And if noise and chaos greets me it's even harder.

This morning was one of those mornings. Luke needed his insulin. My first mistake was that I overslept. Which meant his insulin was late. I pried him out of his hiding space and then held him the wrong way. My cat was not thrilled about this morning ritual and began to struggle.

Mind you he is startled just by the phone and the news in the morning and my sweet eight year old Liam bounded towards us and Luke, stronger than he'd been in months freed himself by scratching the hell out of me.

Fresh out of bed I immediately thought diabetic shock.

I broke out in tears. Like those big fat giant Matt Damon tears in Good Will Hunting. I thought my cat is going to die. My cat is going to die. My cat is going to die.

This, unfortunately set the tone for the day.

I managed to recover. Then I was supposed to take the cat to get his blood sugar taken today. I get him into the cat carrier, I call the vet. They say don't come until tomorrow. I'm thinking, my cat is going to die, my cat is going to die.

As the day wears on it simply gets bleaker and bleaker inside my head. I talk to Missy and feel alone, abandoned, rejected, and like she no longer gives a damn about our friendship. All of this, is a series of big fat lies my diseased brain is telling me.

Does that make me feel any better no.

At this point I start crying. I need help. I need support. I need peace of mind. I need an escape hatch and Missy is resisting the greatest victory lap ever at AOF.

I have an incredible amount of stress on me. I go back to what my why is: To get better!

Get better. Physically.

Get better. Emotionally.

Get better. Physchologically.

Get better at my craft of writing, directing, producing.

Get better at managing my mental illnesses.

Get better at managing my financing.

If possible get better at running.

There are a lot of parallels between running and writing. You get out of them what you put into them.

I haven't run in a long, long time. So this morning I'm going to the park to walk. I plan to earn my marathon medal that I paid for the virtual race.

This will set me up for managing my physical health a whole hell of a lot better than I have recently. I will get better. Because that is my ultimate why.

Get better. Strive one day at a time, one step at a time, one word at a time, one take at a time to get better.

What is your why?

What drives you?

What underlies the simplicity of getting better? Even simpler. For the love it.

Do the accolades drive me? To a degree, I'd be lying if I didn't.

Being rich and famous? My work is about having an audience and building upon that audience.

Making it and defining success for yourself is where you set yourself up for that dreamy feeling when you write the end, call for the martini shot, or cross the finish line.

If you are driven solely by the fact you need to support yourself financially, you will be miserable. Writing will cease to bring you any kind of joy. Filmmaking will cease to have any heart. And running will feel like drudgery.

So whatever your initial why, the underlying one must be a love of doing what you do.

I have friends who say they have endurance and persistence and then complain about working towards something for five years as "hard" and like they're not getting anything out of it.

Here's the reality, there are many of us who love what we do. But art has always been an uneasy marriage of creativity and commerce. Many of us don't want to accept that we have to do far more than just write.

That hustling is a reality of the game. Sending your queries. Establishing on an online presence. Traveling to conventions and festivals and book signings.

You have to be hungry. You have to be ambitious. You have to have talent and passion. But most of all you must have endurance, perseverance and believe your time will come. Because believe me no one else will do it if you don't.

So my fellow creatives, what is your why and what are you going to do with it?

Chapter 10
Once Upon A Time...A Career Takes Shape

Bare with me. Once upon time never runs smoothly. I had what I wanted to say all planned out. But this weekend at Imaginarium something happened that shook me to my core. After the day was done. The vendor hall had closed and all panels were done for the day, me, my best friend and my very good friend, another filmmaker were sitting in the bar waiting for our guest and chatting about the project we were about to collaborate on when our friend Mick Williams fell to the floor and experienced a grand mal seizure. It was horrific and traumatic to witness, but I know for Holly and her son Martin keeping him amongst the living will the Ambulance to their sweet ass time to get there.

I had a mini-confrontation with an old bitch and then proceeded to have a anxiety attack as a result of my senses being overloaded. It took Lee Pennington coming to me and putting his arm around me and saying I like the bang bang but not the shrimp to make the tears finally stop. Thank you Lee!

Fast forward twenty four hours late and I'm sitting in the banquet hall, receiving my awards from 2020. That's three for those of you keeping score and winning runner up for my Recovery Unplugged web series as well as our feature script The Guardian. Talk about a glorious night.

All day today the nominations have been coming through for my scripts at Miracle Makers and X World. It's really been a beautiful thing and they are certainly blessings I am extremely grateful for.

We are two weeks away from AOF MEGAFEST. I am scared, that as a festival director I will fail and let my fam down.

I am exhausted truth be told, but even in the midst of that we are transitioning between just being a production, to being a studio. I never thought I'd find another woman from Kentucky (besides Missy) who was a boss at her own game on her own terms. But amazingly enough at Imaginarium I ran into someone who I've worked with to varying degrees on three previous projects, Kathlene Ashcraft. Those projects being Letters to Daniel, Recovery Unplugged Sizzle Reel, and Nobody's Listening.

Missy and I have been working on our own locally for so long it's ridiculous. But something nice happened this past weekend. I felt embraced to a degree by the Louisville film community.

In particular by two filmmakers, one who wasn't there. Chase Dudley. We agreed to help each other mutually. He's helping with lighting. Herschel Zahnd watched Letters to Daniel and was duly impressed. Demetrius Witherspoon has always had kind words for my work. And a beautiful thing happened in making amends with James Tackett and agreeing to work on a short film and feature film with us.

But onto the master plan.

Healing Hands Entertainment has always been a two man operation. Using The Unlikely Assassin as a dry run my vision became, if it's successful, Girl Power Studios. With me, Missy, Pam, Kathlene, Anabelle, and Lureen at the studio head.

If you had told me it would happen I would have told you that you were crazy. A studio with a 25/18.75x4 split headed by me, surrounded, by other brilliant, creative women, seemed like an unthinkable thing not even that long ago.

I have some Louisville connections I've developed, Chase, Herschel, Haven. It's taken time but people are coming towards me to help make their dreams come true.

I'm super excited about the fall. Thomas Moore and his partner Jay are boarding on Recovery Unplugged and helping us to create a powerful arts and mental health support show for the community in August,

Then the Unlikely Assassin.

Altogether we have nine projects slated over the next 2 to 3 years and the vision is for Girl Power Studios. Run by 5 women. The vision is to happily work with men and women of all stripes.

The five women would include Lureen Wu, Anabelle Munro, Melissa Goodman, Kathlene Ashcraft and me. A German, an Asian, 3 Kentuckians, all Americans working to push the boundaries of their art.

At Imaginarium I sat on a panel of sausages (no offense men) but it was a wholly weird as fuck experience.

As any filmmaker will tell you awards are a beautiful thing and that every step of success should be celebrated.

My first taste of publishing success was 2011. When I signed three contracts in one year. Another Way to Die, No Ordinary Love, and Gladiator, it seemed every five minutes I was celebrating according to my mom.

The truth is no matter how miniscule to someone else, steps forward do need to be celebrated.

I have to say, having 29 books published, 11 of them nominated, many of them award winning, I could rest on my laurels but that has never been my way and my hard earned wisdom should be neither should you.

That was in 2011. This past February marked the ten year publication anniversary.

In 2014 I made my first (seen) film, a documentary, Letters to Daniel. It travelled to 5 festivals and was accepted by all of them, won at 4 of them.

For three years it was Conglomeration, Imaginarium, and Indie Gathering. In 2016 AOF and I found each other. And suddenly it wasn't just about being a festival goer. That career I had always dreamed of having was a real possibility.

A career was indeed taking shape, my parents didn't understand why I had to travel or why I had to spend so much money on a career that wasn't paying any dividends at the time.

But here I am on the cusp of all I've ever wanted.

I often hear: I have no time, I'm married, I've got kids. Those aren't reasons. Those are excuses. I have no more time than you do.

This career that was taking shape. What does it take? A relentless, implacable drive to create. Hustle with ambition. And the patience and perseverance to trust that the dream will come true.

So before moving on to the next chapter choose your project book or screenplay and decide whether or not you want to sell the rights or whether or not you want to make it yourself into a film.

Chapter 11
Your Turn to Fade In

So you decided to wanted to write a movie. Which means I have to break a few things to you. In order to see that brilliant spec script of yours on the silver screen, you're going to need to at least be a producer/writer. Don't like what you hear? That's the reality right now in the industry.

Some of you may itch to direct, and expect a studio or production company to invest millions of dollars in you, an unknown, unproven quantity.

My advice think only of the story, but think of how you can do it for very little. Limited locations. Limited cast.

Up until Letters to Daniel all of my films had been done for under one thousand dollars. All 22 of them. Letters to Daniel however was a seven year adventure. From popular blog, to multiple volumes of memoirs to proof of concept documentary to script to narrative film it was the best of times and the hardest of times. But as Tom Hanks said in A League of Their Own, it's the hard that makes it great.

So let's begin at the beginning.

With the script.

To fade in or not to fade in.

I am going to ask you, before you begin, how tough are you? What kind of endurance do you have? Are you waiting for your Lana Turner in a soda shop moment (which never happens)? Or are you willing to hustle? Are you ready to work your ass off with no guarantee of your script going to screen?

Here's the brutal truth. *No one is going to produce your first script except for you. Or someone professionally close to you.* You want to direct and it's your first feature. Same thing. You have to do it. You have to commit. For me and Missy it was our homerun swing. We weren't going to have another opportunity and we had to hit it out of the park.

The amazing thing is, we did.

And I believe anyone can. It just take a lot of fucking hard work. It starts with two little words. Fade in.

When it comes down to it, you can tell any story you want, it just depends on what your goals are. Truth be told all screenwriters have that dream of standing on the grandest stage of them all.

Saying I'd like to thank the academy isn't part of the dream, for me would be a lie. But to say making a movie isn't gratifying in and of itself would be a lie too. Focus Amy. The first step is figuring out what you want to be. A screenwriter? A screenwriter/producer? A screenwriter/director? Or a triple threat?

I speak from a triple threat's view point. My way is not the only way to write a script. In fact when it comes to shopping a script for representation and production there is such a thing as industry format. Final Draft is the industry standard for screenwriting software.

There are several kinds, but I highly recommend you invest in it if you are serious about making a career in the industry you need it. If you are someone who enjoys making their own films this might not be as crucial. But I highly recommend you get it. Unless you have a chromebook. Then I recommend Celtx.

Now that we have that settled, what kind of story do you want to tell.

Drama?

Romance?

Action?

Suspense?

Horror?

Crime?

Sci-fi? Fantasy?

The world is your oyster at the beginning of a story. Generally speaking, if you are an indie producer/writer/director, for your first feature film, your broke. And I don't just mean broke or shoestring on Hollywood's terms. I'm talking you are going to utilize every resource you have. Such as your family's house, your family's car, your family's church. Do you know someone who owns a coffee shop, a mom and pop restaurant?

Do you have friends who have a beautiful, upper middle class home that could pass for a wealthy person's home?

Use all of it in the script.

Whatever is free keep your producer brain on while writing. And always remember, the writer is king. The truth is no one in Hollywood will tell you that. But no one in the industry has a job without you.

So what genre did you pick?

I picked Drama for my first excursion. Not only that, I had, and still have, a co-screenwriter. Initially things such as a bus ride and a grease fire was in our first produced narrative feature. Even a clip from the Emmy's with Maurice Benard. But the truth is we didn't have the money to include them.

So, before a scene was ever shot, all of that was cut from the script. Which would force our editor to get creative down the road.

Our very script was a romantic drama. Some don't realize those are often the cheapest yet the most emotionally rewarding films to make.

Of course, there's the documentary. That is how I honed my filmmaking skills. Little overhead and it can be about almost anything. As I wrote countless short and feature scripts I shot nearly as many docs, music videos, micro films, and short narratives.

All of this merely stoked the creative fire to want to do a feature, one which I would direct. Like you see in the movies.

The story I decided to tell was my own. A true story based on my struggle from bipolar breakdown to bestseller. From blog to memoir to script to doc to screen as a narrative feature it took seven years. So when you write this story you better love it first and foremost.

Did I love the story of my life? I would have to say I was passionate about it. Because as soon as the idea popped in my head I had deep burning fire in my mind, body, and soul to tell that story. So much so I took it to Missy, my co-writer. She said, let me think about it.

Of course, I gave her, her space but the desire to tell our story was so strong I was compelled to start writing before Missy ever signed off on it.

I really don't advise this. You better know your writing partner very, very well before attempting a hire wire act like this. Now that we're passed the actual making of the film and am successful, she thinks, jeez, that's just Amy. Had I told her what I was doing at the time she would have dug her heels in and it would have never gotten made.

Fade In:

EXT. MANSION-DAY

A sexy 40 year old MAN observes a 40 something woman dancing.

Above is a prompt to any genre film you can think of. Now open your mind, crank up the music and start telling your story that you've always dreamed of telling.

Chapter 12
A Break

I'm taking a timeout here. This last week, July 25 through August 1st I helped run a festival. Normally that's not anything to sneeze at anyway, but this festival was special. First of all it was the AOF Megafest. Second of all the big man, the creator of the festival was down. He was and still is as of this moment hospitalized and fighting for his life. His last communications to his family was that the AOF Megafest must go on. And all the festival directors who could make it did make it.

Certain manipulators were amongst us and people using the AOF in a negative way were there. Fortunately those elements were rooted out at their source and will not be there again.

Shane was a bona fide superhero on theater tech issues. Anabelle rose to the occasion, a super boss anyway she truly earned her title the Queen of AOF, Lureen was her super assistant, while each of them ran their own ancillary festivals, TMIF and Las Vegas Asian Film Awards, which are umbrella-ed under the AOF Megafest.

Even though I have a festival involved, I feel as if I failed them. My anxiety topped out several times leaving me useless. So I just made sure everyone had coffee, food, water, and tried to tend to my part of the festival, Conquering Disabilities with Film.

So what does this have to with making a film. Shouldn't I be telling you about film festivals AFTER I tell you about how to make a film?

I tell you this now because I was operating without my partner in crime. And while I love AOF it normally forces me to utilize all my coping skills anyway. Running a festival nestled amongst the greatest festival I have ever attended proved especially challenging without my caregiver, and the fact our venerable leader was in the hospital fighting for his life.

But thanks to the real AOF Family pulling together, a miracle happened. The festival went off. Del's last communication to his family before being taken to the hospital was that this year's AOF was to happen, by hook or by crook.

This is where I pause and say, working a festival can be a thankless task. But in this case the incredible effort put forth was worth it. Who we were doing it for and why was always in the forefront of our minds.

Still even with Del on a ventilator and certain mishagos going on it was controlled chaos. And even with people finally knowing Del was fighting for his life, there were tons of content creators complaining, criticizing Theresa Weston and could not be satisfied.

There was tension within the festival too.

A calculating bitch, and two others who did not know how to mesh with the group as a whole. But somehow, some way we survived. We didn't come out of it unscathed. There were accusations of home cooking. Across the different festivals, between film and writing, outright winning and runner-ups, there were nineteen awards to be had.

Now that I'm a festival director, going forward, it looks like for headache purposes, and the integrity question (even though we have judges with great taste) , no Megafest festival director will be allowed to enter any of the individual festivals.

Initially this made me sad.

Every award I've won at AOF has been earned. Winning at AOF or any of it's subsidary festivals is like running with the bulls in Pamplona. Exhilarating, Del Weston has a knack for picking winners.

He encouraged me to dream big and believe in my talent. Because he believed there was magic in me.

So going forward, I will not enter Megafest festivals. Not because they're not worthy, but because they are. I will use them to four wall my work, to qualify it for prestigious awards such as the Film Independent Spirit Awards, SAG, WGA, DGA, and the Oscars or the Emmys.

I will pivot towards film markets, Film-Com and AFM and others with an eye towards distribution. I have team that includes the likes of Anabelle Munro, Lureen Wu, Missy Goodman, Isaac Hernandez, and now Martin Glover & Deborah Watson.

Del, Theresa, Simone, Auguste are my heroes and they my family. Through them I will be able to support and nurture Megafest, by running Conquering Disabilities w/Film in order to help others like me on this path.

Chapter 13
Now That You've Typed FADE OUT

What comes after finishing the script? Putting the team together that will get your script made. Early on this will mean YOU and maybe one or two others do everything at this stage. sChances are you will have cut your teeth on music videos, micro films, maybe even some short narratives and documentaries.

The real test comes, when you go to make your first feature.

Even for a bad movie to get made it takes everything going to plan and when it doesn't it's up to the director and his team to get things back on track. For a movie to turn out good, even great, is just icing on the cake. And to be honest you just don't know which way your film is going to turn out. There are just too many variables.

So, I'm talking to everyone out there swinging for the fences. A professional career in the film industry is not for the faint of heart. As it says show/business. But if you don't find joy in the process storytelling there's no reason you should be at this. And if you don't know the concept of the hustling that is part and parcel of the business and you don't want to do everything that is needed to stack the odds in your favor, checkout now. If you are about to give me 100 different excuses as to why you can't, then this business IS NOT for you.

They say thick skin. Or this business will chew you up and spit you out. You better love storytelling with all that is within you. I mean you better have a burning passion that can sustain you. Ambition tempered by humanity. And the ability to persevere and persist.

So first thing you do, find a producer. How?

Film festivals. You can't overestimate how valuable these places are as networking tools. I took my scripts and a zero budget doc to some smaller festivals and grew in my ability to pitch and network.

And that's what smaller fests are for. For growing your team and making smaller films that allow you to learn by doing so. Unfortunately, in true indie film, early on you will have to pretzel yourself to fit everyone's schedule.

If you're like me in the beginning there was fucking you and maybe one person, if that. I became a director because no one wanted to make my movie, Letters to Daniel. Because at the heart of it I'm a writer before I am anything else.

I come from a family of teachers. My Aunt Sue is a teacher, my cousin Jill is a teacher, my MOM is a teacher, my sister Brandy is a teacher, my dad before he became a public defender, was a substitute teacher.

I never saw myself as a teacher. However, I have had several mentors. Many of them male. So I hope with this book I may not teacher you, but I might plant some seeds to mentor you.

Travel and build your team.

The next question you need to ask yourself is, at what level do you want to work? True indie. I call true indie, NO STARS, NO MONEY, NO EXPLOSIONS, NO FX. Pure grit. Do you want to make a calling card film? One that is true indie, but looks and sounds magnificent, like cinematic release without any stars.

Timeline of how I built the Letters to Daniel team.

1. May 2013 created the Letters to Daniel blog
2. October 2013 release Letters to Daniel Memoir Vol 1
3. February 2014 release Vol 2
4. March 2014 made the $345 budget proof of concept documentary Letters to Daniel.
5. February 2015 co-wrote the narrative script.
6. January 2016 release the complete revised edition with 2/ 3rd's new material of Letters to Daniel memoir.
7. September 2018 go into pre-production on the narrative

feature film Letters to Daniel.
8. June 2019 go into production.
9. October 2019 a finished film.

I will skip the talk about distribution right now, but allow
me a caveat.

Distribution should be a part of the whole process. But I don't
want to overwhelm you.

As you see in the above timeline it took quite a few years to
accomplish it. If you are a writer, and please, do it first for the joy. The
odds in this industry are long. And for pete's sake, don't be that diva
who waits. Waits for their career to just start. Wait to be discovered.
Wait for life to start happening.

From 2013 to 2019 I was constantly hustling. That's part of the
game.

2016 was a turning point. That was the year Action On Film and I
discovered one another and it was love at first sight.

You just need one person who believes in you. And while you
must always believe in yourself first, and take action to prove it, I had
someone travelling the path with me. MEGAFEST introduced me to
the Westons.

They completely changed my life. I now am developing into the
dream filmmaker that I always dreamed that I would. All because I
swung for the fences.

AOF changed me in that I had been through some traumatic shit
with some shady characters and some broken ones not so shady. They
picked me up, dusted me off and showered me with their love and
belief that I could do this with the tools they would give me.

It was there I blossomed and truly came into my own. I found
my editor in Clint Gaige and my cinematographer in Mark Maness.
They, coupled with Valyo Gennoff, and Brandon X Bell from Indie

Gathering, and Ginny and Megan through Thomas at Imaginarium took the dream of a film to a completed film.

When you have bipolar disorder like I do, it's a miracle that you get out of bed in the morning. Del Weston was like a father to me. One that went all in on my success. Believed I could succeed as director. Saw me as a director. Saw me as a writer. Saw me as a full blooded artist and advocate with something to say.

And what happened, even with covid-19, it took the festival circuit by storm. Winning 52 awards and over 70 nominations. Secured two streaming deals (Saltflix & Reel Women's Network) and a library distribution deal (Green Apple Entertainment).

Now I have what I call the Creative Avengers team. Isaac Hernandez, Joshua Carpenter, Marvin Glover, Anabelle Munro, Lureen Wu, Kathlene Ashkraft, John Spalding, and Melissa Goodman.

This year I had my most successful screening of any film that I've ever made.

Letters to Daniel screened to a packed house. Had a lively Q & A. It received eight nominations, one win, one runner up. My parents were there. In short, even with covid my dreams were not stopped. Everything Del had said has come true.

Writing about him keeps him fresh in my mind. He has enabled countless creators to come together make their dreams come true.

I should tell you, starting with smaller festivals is a way to go. And I'll detail that when I get into distribution facts and myths.

Homework, it does and doesn't matter what you shoot on in the beginning. Just as long as you know what you're doing. For your first film shoot on a smartphone if you've never handled a camera before. It's more forgiving, now go out and find your production team going forward.

Chapter 14
Arriving On Set

So, you've written the script. Did all the annoying, yet necessary paperwork. Hired your cast and crew. Secured locations. And put together your post-production team.

Are you itching to get on set? Scream action and roll sound? Prove to the world and Hollywood or Indiewood you have what it takes?

Most feature film shoots last, indie wise can last as little as one week to four weeks. Cost as little as zero dollars to 250k. I shot Letters to Daniel in six days for six grand. We raised 2k and 2k came directly out of my pocket and 2k came directly out of Missy's account.

If you put in the legwork to get to this point, you might not be working by yourself. For my first feature film I had 9 crew members, many who pulled double and triple duty as part of the cast as well.

I had close to forty cast members.

The set was what one would call organized chaos. Surviving and getting the scenes on film. A set is a juggling act as the director it is incumbent on you to see to it everything is as it's supposed to be.

It won't always be. And in intervals the shit will hit the proverbial fan. I highly recommend having to a killer 1AD and a highly organized UPM. If you can find a qualified script supervisor or someone willing to learn the position before and on the job those are below the line crew member that will make your life oh so much easier.

Find the AD and the Line Producer aka Unit Production Manager.

They are lifesavers.

Do you have someone to run slate? Sound? Do you have someone to do make-up and hair?

People will tell you that you have to go to film school to establish yourself. The thing that comes out of film school are the potential relationships you make. The producer attached to Letters to Daniel:

the Series, Marvin Glover, I met through AOF Megafest. He was a consulting producer on my friend Anabelle Munro's film the Weight of Perfection.

Marvin is an amazing man. And I look forward to having him on set. This is a big production I'm trying to get going. He understands what I want for it and he doesn't think it's laughable. Which I find amazing because he came upon me when I was an emotional wreck after learning my cat had a seizure and I was over a thousand miles away from him unable to do anything for him. Thank god for my mom and dad taking him to the hospital. Even though he is expensive he is worth it.

I'm sure Marvin will be expensive. Marvin Glover is a brilliant producer and is working on several projects. They include one with Sean Kanan of Karate Kid Part 3 fame, aka AJ Quartermaine of General Hospital, Emmy winning producer of Studio City, and bestselling author, including the Way of the Cobra.

I hold out the slimmest of hopes that Marvin can get my feature film, Letters to Daniel to Daniel Craig. I may never know what Daniel thinks of it but maybe I can fancy the fact he's seen it.

Anyway, be super organized. The only reason I was able to achieve the impossible with the film was because I was determined to do it and not allow anyone or anything to stop me.

That's the way you have to be too.

As my mentor said, people fail everyday in this industry just by not getting started. Then, by not following through.

You have a dream of directing a movie, then by god get out there and do it. But be hyper organized and in order to that you need a script supervisor. Some times you will have to where multiple hats yourself. And in the beginning many of these positions will be filled by one or two of the same people.

As you grow as an artist, and in the ability to network, you will gain more people willing to work with you. More skilled and more talented as you go and you will learn.

The making of your first film is a glorious and wonderful thing. At least my experience with Broken, my first narrative short, was. There was a lot of raw talent, all of us very green. And even though the producer on Broken turned out to be a very sick woman and mentally unstable she was a very steadying influence on that set.

We shot twenty five pages in one day.

We became a family.

And my lead male actor, Brandon X Bell, became more like my brother. We became creative partners in crime. We've done three movies together and are about to do our fourth together in March.

For me I cut my teeth on documentaries, micro films, music videos, and short narratives while pushing to get my feature film made. Pieces for the Letters to Daniel shoot came together through the creative writing convention Imaginarium, Indie Gathering, and AOF aka Del and Theresa Weston.

Friends may come and go, but people like Del are one of a kind. As a mentor, as a friend, as a cheerleader, in this business there will never be another like him. Losing him is the one of the hardest things I've ever experienced. Since it happened on August 24, 2021 its barely been a week and feels very raw.

But I was privileged to know him for years. In those five years he irrevocably changed my life for the good by believing in me. Everyone needs a Del Weston in their life, but not everyone gets one.

Having Missy. Having Del. Having Theresa. Having them changed my life and now I have opportunities I wouldn't have otherwise had. Del taught me it's okay to dream giant sized dreams.

When you commit to your first film, that's what you're doing. And it's a heady feeling shouting action on your first film. Remember that feeling as it will have to sustain you through the lean times.

But take it from me, it's worth it and it makes the success all the more sweet when it happens.

Chapter 15

Redefining Success & Learning to Keep Your Eyes On Your Own Lane

I have a dear friend. I won't mention their name, but let's just say they take other's success personally. Granted, she's had a hand dealt to her, but the reality all of us certain things drive us.

I have another friend which like the other one, are driven by the desperation for money. Granted, both of them are in the same boat as me where it comes to money. I have conversations with them that say I need money. Come to think of it, a third colleague and friend is driven by hardship too.

I'm not saying making money or wanting to be solvent is bad or wrong. But the truth is making a movie, writing a book, or whatever and aiming for success is great. But what does success mean to you.

Honestly, you better love what you're doing. And you better know going in the world owes you shit. Success is what you decide it is. And gratitude better factor into it.

This is how my thought process goes.

I survive bipolar disorder on a daily basis.

I manage my diabetes. These are life or death successes. Having earned the right to be happy and just create for the joy of it is incredibly important. Completing projects I start is another form of success.

I see people covet what other people have and all it does eat them up from the inside out. I mean letting something burn or live rent free in your mind does you no good. Find your joy. Keep it. Fight for it. Don't confuse your hustle for the business side of things for the love of what you do.

The love of what you do has to drive you.

That doesn't mean wanting accolades is bad.

That doesn't mean wanting money to live without having to worry about bills, a roof over your head, or knowing where your next meal is coming from is bad either.

Resenting what others have, assuming they're not busting their asses, or assuming you deserve what someone else has worked for is a fruitless endeavor.

In other words, keep your eyes on your own lane. Define what you want out of your career. Define how bad you want it. Now put your blinders on and focus.

Chapter 16
Post Production

They say a film is made three times. First, when it's written. Then when it's filmed. And finally when it's handed over to an editor.

There's not telling how long a project, from original concept, to finished film will take to complete. For me from blog to memoir to documentary to narrative script to finished feature film took seven years.

I love making movies. I hate pre-production. And the wait for a finished film is hard. But when it all comes together, there's nothing sweeter. Let me tell. When your film exceeds all expectations, your dream coming true, there's nothing like it.

Right now I'm putting deliverables together for the distribution company. They are keen to get Letters to Daniel out on the multiple streaming platforms.

Letters to Daniel has been a spring board but it wasn't without its trials and tribulations on its path to completion.

Upon first inspection the sound was troubled.

God bless our sound people. They were not the most experienced in sound. But without them there would be no film. But they certainly made for an interesting time in post.

First of all, I had a brilliant editor. It helps to have someone who appreciates the material and wants the best for it. And most of all knows that you want it to be all that it can be and will serve the story first, which is what you want to serve first.

We initially recorded at -36dbz. If you know anything about sound design and technology you know that's pretty much a fucking disaster. You should record at -6dbz. But somehow the other half of my brilliant post production team, Valyo Gennoff, my composer and sound editor was able to sweeten and rescue the sound and make it passable.

The turn around time for Clint Gaige and Valyo were just amazing. We finished production late June, and had a finished film by October. By October 3 I had a manager (unfortunately we parted ways. It was amicable. Her areas of expertise were not mine. Reality shows and wrestling stars and horror films). She wanted to turn Letters to Daniel into a reality series. But no one in my life wanted to be featured on television.

Not many people can bear the honesty and grief that Letters to Daniel deals in. Couched in a narrative film it can be incredibly inspirational. Documentaries can be Devine. I have done both. Now it is at Netflix (a pitch deck and pilot) awaiting a greenlight.

Folks I beg of you not to give up on your material. And if it begins to look like it won't get made unless you do it, then quit your bitching and just fricking do it.

God knows I wasted many years waiting for the "perfect" time to do anything. Including realizing I would have to make a feature film all by myself from start to finish in order to make my career jump from festival darling to mainstream success.

For post production I picked an amazing team.

And there were lessons I learned on the set of Letters to Daniel. In my early films I edited them myself. I wasn't very good, and I was using a very basic editing program. It certainly wasn't pro quality.

However in this business you make the most of what you can. And every crappy film I made I got a little better. And then I connected with some great people at Imaginarium, Indie Gathering, and AOF Megafest. Those three festivals I built my cast and crew and post production from.

This industry, if it's about anything, it's about relationships and partnerships. There are people you can trust and people you can't. And when you find the people you can. Hold on tight, there are too many counterfeits to play games with the real deal.

Post production is exciting.

You make a film three times.

Once when you write. Again when you shoot it. And finally when you edit it.

Be confident in your vision and be able to articulate it. But Godssakes do listen to your editor and trust them. Get someone with experience who will serve the story, but be sure to fight the right fights. Don't die on a stupid hill.

To wit, I just watched Project Greenlight. I used to love the romance of the story of Matt Damon and Ben Affleck. Now I'm disenchanted with them. The person they picked? A privileged white asshole who acted so wholly unprofessionally after being GIVEN 3 million dollars to make a film OMG. By the second episode I was secretly praying Effie Brown would fucking cold cock him into oblivion.

They brought her one for diversity and god bless her she called them all on their white privileged bullshit.

I soldiered on through the eight episodes and was ready to break my computer by the end of it.

Needless to say.

Have a vision.

Maintain your integrity.

Be a real leader.

Be collaborative.

Create a family like atmosphere where everyone is going to be giving their best in the name of your project.

So what gain you glean from my experience?

Invest as much in your post production team as you do everything else because they are the ones who will save your ass in the end. My editor is amazing. Clint Gaige is a successful film and tv director in his own right.

I met him at AOF in 2016.

That festival changed my life. There are people and places that will change yours too. So needless to say. Network.

Network. Network. Network.

That's your homework.

Find a way to meet someone face to face. And see the difference it makes upon your career.

A great post production team can me the difference between a success and being an also ran. Also, the ass you kick today on the way up is the ass you kiss on the way down tomorrow.

Chapter 17
The Pitch Deck

The pitch deck. Oh the pitch deck. The beautiful, cumbersome, tedious, but when done right it is oh so glorious. What do I mean by that? Say you've made your "proof of concept", written your pilot or feature, you'll need a pitch deck. They can cost upwards of thousands of dollars. Unless you meet some ridiculously talented individual at a film festival like I did, get to know them and work together on projects where there's a give and take.

Pitch decks are designed to convey the tone and atmosphere of the world you're script/film takes place in, give comparables, ideal cast, and the production team.

It is hard laborious work to get it just right.

You need someone with skills or someone who knows your vision.

You should have an artistic rendering of the characters. Pictures and photos of actual desired cast.

A pitch deck conveys visually what you intend to do and allows investors and producers to quantify that. In other words a great pitch deck can help you pick up key people along the way who can help you get things done.

A great tool to practice and teach yourself on is Canva.

Canva is photoshop for dummies. It has all the tips and tricks of Photoshop without such a steep learning curve.

I've been working on it for a year and I'm starting to produce some nice stuff. For two different festivals and a series. My previous decks by the ridiculously talented Anabelle Munro have fetched me a distribution deal and development deal. Not too shabby.

Anabelle is brilliant. And is part of my heart.

So is Lureen.

So are so many people.

Like Del and Theresa Weston. Like my parents. Like everyone in my writing circle. Like Pam and Missy.

If you ever wonder why at awards shows everyone gets the I love yous and wants to thank everyone it's because if it was a joyous experience and a labor of love for all concern from writers to producers to actors to director, to all aspects of the crew, there is only one trophy and they're up there repping the whole shebang.

Pitch decks are the first visual representation of your dream. They are the first step to realizing your script as a show or film.

If you use Canva appropriately, and utilize your imagination beyond the written word. You multiply your chances of realizing the dream of a studio produced version of your dream.

I've yet to make a multimillion dollar film or show. But I do have a limited series in development, and feature film that upon completion will receive distribution. Letters to Daniel is in the hands of Netflix producers as we speak. I have secured two meetings at the American Film Market in a couple of weeks. And I recently inked deals with a manager and a literary agent.

At this level you need pitch decks.

You need beautiful pitch decks.

You need at least a deck that skillfully convey your vision.

There's a quote I love from my recovery. "Progress, not perfection."

Another one is "Opportunity is hard work in disguise."

Pitch decks are incredibly hard, but worthwhile work. They can get you that breakthrough contact that will elevate you to the next level.

Who do you show the deck to?

Creative executives. Producers. Executive Producers. Studio Executives. Financiers.

Pitch decks quantify your vision to these decision makers. Please remember something. These meeting only usually last ten minutes and it's on to the next. If this time doesn't work out there will be a next time.

You never know what will break you through to the mainstream. And there is no one path, I think William Goldman said it best when he said, "Nobody knows anything."

People often dream of being discovered ala Lana Turner at the soda shop. That in and of itself is an Urban Legend. It didn't happen folks. It doesn't happen. No one is plucked from obscurity and made famous.

It's all fucking hard work.

Meets opportunity.

And capitalizing on it.

And a righteous pitch deck and script will take you more places than just a script, and only a pitch will take you when your first trying to break in. Keep the faith if it can happen for me it can happen for you.

Chapter 18

Distribution Part I: The Film Festival Circuit

My journey to distribution is a unique one, as are journeys to distribution

on are. It starts before a word of the script/screenplay is written. It goes back to that nebulous thing called your vision.

When I created the Letters to Daniel blog I had no intention of it being anything other than a blog. Not a book, not a film, not a play. And certainly not a one woman show. But it has become all these things. The play needs to be workshopped. The series needs to be produced, but the berween the blog, book, and film I dreamed of and manifested them into existence. Visualize, put it out into the universe, and put action behind it. Write, learn your craft, and network. Shoot your film. Network some more. Shop your film. Hold the boat. What is distribution?

In the past it was movie theaters.

Then VOD.

The television broadcasts.

Now you have cable networks. Television. And the streamers.

There are countless streamers.

Before I get your head spinning let's define what distribution is. Distribution is the dissemination of your film to the movie going audience. The definition of that has radically changed to include Netflix streaming, Hulu and countless others. Thing is traditional distribution still exists and self distribution is easier than ever. What you have to narrow it down in order to give you focus, is how do you want your film to be seen.

For some it's a DVD on the shelf in your local Target or Wal-Mart. Others it's getting on Netflix. And for others they still dream of theatrical releases and premieres. Academy Awards and Emmys, and yes the Golden Globes.

Some decide film festivals and a festival run where there film markets contained in the festival are the best way to go.

The networking thing became my super power. That combined with constant writing. Constantly shaving off the rough edges to hone my craft. Am I writing with a sale in mind? No. Am I filming with a goal of a sale in mind well, if I'm completely honest yes.

But life in the industry no guarantee of pluck you from obscurity success. I believe if you want something bad enough you will do whatever it takes short of selling your soul to the devil and/or breaking the law. And trust me, there will be times when you will be tempted to do both. Fortunately, I have a partner in this that won't allow me to do too many stupid things.

We've had our fair share of hard knocks. Some due to life. Some due to illness. And still others due to youth and stupidity. But it is with implacable persistence and refusing to give up that a lot of these things are happening.

When you do go out on the circuit, be purposeful in your submissions approach. Have a game plan. Research the festival. Find out if your vision for what a film festival can do lines up.

Ironically, I was told to enter mental health festivals. Not a single acceptance. That's not bitterness. That wasn't, on the face it, bad advice either. For some reason our visions and messages don't align.

So I entered a lot of festivals. I never entered Sundance with the Letters to Daniel film. I tried entering their screenwriting lab with it and was unsuccessful. I've been largely unsuccessful in the top tier festivals. Basically I get told my writing sucks. And when I get coverage (it's rare that in the climb up that I could afford it), they often eviscerated my work for it's own good.

Letters to Daniel: The Motion Picture was truly my springboard moment. It got me the real deal representation. It opened doors to meetings with Netflix and Cowan Entertainment.

And finally another dream is coming true. A literary agent for my novel and memoir writing.

So how did I do it?

Hopefully I'm articulating the most important lesson. Which is love what you do to the point of obsession. Be implacably persistent. Write madly, as if you were running out of time. Listening to and watching Hamilton makes me think of how I handle my career. And like I feel the clock ticking because I wandered the bipolar desert for fifteen years, playing (writing) alone in the sandbox being allowed to explore, fantasize, and use my imagination to tell the stories I wanted to tell. I wanted to be seen as a skilled writer, but I knew I would need to keep writing. Knock on doors. And if they didn't open, keep kicking at them until they gave or I did, realizing that there were plenty of other doors and windows of opportunity to check out.

Distribution in other words should always be factored in at the very beginning of formation of the script. Story is King. Writer is King. But the vision must include where you plan to show it.

Do you want to mount an Oscar campaign?

Then you must account for that too.

So the question you must ask answer where distribution is concerned, Where do I want my movie to screen, and who is my target audience?

Know the story like the back of your hand.

Know your target audience.

Know what platform of distribution you want.

And on to the next.

Chapter 19

Distribution Part 2: The Act of Putting Together the Deliverables

This chapter will be really brief.

Okay, not that brief.

Only to say putting deliverables together is every bit as important arduous as writing the script, putting the funds together, shooting the script, editing the film and producing the final cut with a score to die for.

Distribution, is the end game.

When the world finally experiences your blood, sweat, and tears, and you sit whatever theater and experience it with a crowd of movie goers and they stand up and cheer for your vision. There is simply nothing like it.

Like I said, short.

Part II
I Just Want to Be A Writer

Chapter 20
Once Upon A Time...

Once upon a time there was a writer. She came up in the golden age of publishing. I came up during the golden age of publishing. February of 2011 I received my first legitimate publication contract.

I had seen Casino Royale, the essential reboot of James Bond with Daniel Craig. It. Changed. My. Life.

I needed a muse.

I needed a genre.

I needed to be able to envision a hero that I could carry in my hip pocket and take from story to story and fall in love with for 50,000 words. And Daniel Craig, and his myriad of performances and characters began to immediately feed the engine.

Telling stories and crafting adventures for fictional folk has been a part of my life since I was very young. Five years old, I was a confirmed book worm, television junkie, and movie going fan.

So when I was in my thirties and I watch Daniel Craig out of the water buff and cut and looking like the ultimate sexy spy. One that I, as a woman, responded to in a very visceral, very real way.

He had not only, brought James Bond to life, and he set the bar way higher by *redefining* the role.

All of us have those moments in our lives. Ones that deeply and radically change us. Moments that, for better or worse, reset your course and you become a different human being and artist you would have been even five seconds ago.

If you are a writer in this day and age you will need to have a working knowledge of the business side, or you will need a partner whose drive is unlike yours. It's one thing to dream and it's another to have ambition, and another still to do the constant work to manifest into being. Meaning you can't be just a writer.

There is no such thing anymore.

But yes there is you protest.

To me people who say they can't or won't. You want to be "discovered". The reality is you are discovered many times in this industry. And you must help those forces along. It is not enough just to write anymore. You have to hustle and be your own hero to.

Once Upon A Time…

When I was five years old I started writing my own stories.

I was a fan of college basketball and horses. Truly a girl of Kentucky.

So what kind of writer do you want to be?

Author? Screenwriter? Poet? Podcast writer? Playwright?

Let's focus on the first one mentioned. You want to be a published author. You want to be a NYT Bestselling author? That's a little more complicated. Let's start with the basics. In order to be an author, you must have written and published something.

You want to write a novel. Let's do what everyone does and begin at the beginning.

And in the beginning you are a writer. Every writer needs a social media presence. It's just a matter of fact.

I can here the whining and gnashing of teeth now. But I'm not interested in doing that. But all I need to do is write. Folks, you need readers. And you need to engage them. As you are writing you need to build and gather an audience who will buy your book ultimately and run and tell everyone around them about your beloved book.

I was told in the beginning that I needed at least a personal website, twitter and facebook. Yes Facebook and Mark Zuckerberg are evil, but if you keep your eyes one your own line. Talk about your art and avoid politics and don't just accept rando friends who are not who they say they are, Facebook can be a relatively good place to be.

Twitter seems to be politics run amuck, your superstar authors seem to be there. And celebrities are on there and there's no telling what publishers, cover artists, or editors who you might connect with.

I have had two wildly successful blogs. One on writing itself and one about my journey with bipolar disorder addressed to Daniel Craig. I am now hosted by G1NBC (a global independent media company) where it comes to my blogging.

What I learned is, whatever you blog about, it should come from the heart. It should reflect you. Be honest, be human, be generous and be authentic where your journey is concerned.

I would also recommend hooking into instagram and be on the lookout for Copper a new social media platform for writers invented by a writer to connect authors and readers.

So you want to write a novel. Where do you start? First question to answer, are you a plotter, pantster, or are you that rare combo of plotter and pantster, a plantster?

A plotter is someone who outlines everything, researches to the tenth degree, and writes detailed backstory for each and every character.

A pantster jumps off at the storytelling point with a line of dialogue. A character. An image and makes the drive with their headlights on the whole, everything just barely illuminated, allowing them to discover and experience the story as they go.

A plantster is a combination of the two.

Writing is like a muscle. It must be built. And building a novel for me is pure joy. It's like falling off the face of the earth and escaping to another world. Even if it's one that reflects our own. Love seems to course through it.

And love is the most enjoyable thing to write about. Be it tragic, melodramatic, literary, puritanical, true, or sexy. Love inspires and adds to all.

Snap it into any genre and you add depth to the characters. Motivation becomes more personal.

If you're tackling the novel break it up. And for all of us who know how lonely and isolating a writer's life can be checkout nanowrimo.org they do several writing events over the course of the year and they may be able to help you get across the finish line and write THE END on your initial draft.

Ask yourself:

What is/are the genres of my story?

Who are the main players in this tale?

What is the core of their journey together?

And what type of a writer are you?

If you can answer these questions then you are ready to start your novel writing journey.

Chapter 21
Building A Novel Brick by Brick

The first time I read a book I was five years old. I had finished all my school work and was given the choice what to do with my time. So I went to the back of the room and there was this record player. Next to it was a book with a play along record. Movies distilled into small picture books.

What I remembered most was being enraptured by the written word.

A clever little trick my librarian used to play was only play part one of a movie adapted from a book, forcing us if we wanted to know how it ended to seek out that book and check it out in order to know how it ended.

She groomed me into the perfect bookworm. I loved stories and I loved books. Some of my favorite authors were and continue to be Ray Bradbury, Kurt Vonnegut, Madeline L'Engle, Sue Grafton, Scott O'Dell, Katherine Patterson, Judy Blume, to name a few.

When I was introduced to the idea of being a writer myself, I was quite young. Around 5 or 6. Becoming an author fascinated me. Of course every child who dreams of being an author dreams of being rich and traveling around the world and doing book signings.

People dream that the success and the discovery of their work will just magically happen. This is an echo of the Lana Turner at soda shop urban legend. It simply doesn't happen that way. I'll tell you how it does work.

Attack the market.

Be someone who is constantly grinding and creating.

I said brick by brick. Some people plot. Some people don't. And others fall in the doing a bit of both categories.

For me it doesn't really start with a plot.

It starts with something a bit more nebulous. A feeling. That indescribable excitement when you know a story is coming but you don't know quite what it is.

I don't need to know how the story ends to start. Don't get me wrong I know some people do. That's just not my process. Before one can be published, one must write the book. The first thing you must have? A hero who desires/wants something above all else. The second? Someone who, at all costs desires to stop them in attaining it.

A hero or anti-hero. A villain. A guide. I always have an anti-hero with heroic qualities. And if you're writing a romance make your woman compelling. For me ripped bodice love stories are weird male fantasies.

I digress.

You don't have to know how the journey is going to end to start writing your story. Usually I have the above ingredients cooking in the cauldron.

Sometimes I will hear music and it will inspire me or send searching for characters and story that it triggers within me. Still others it's a film and the entire presentation that draw me to tell another vision of that.

Different things stir the muse.

Point is you have different tools. Stephen King likened plot to a jackhammer. Sure you'll get to the story but you'll miss the nuances, layers, and nooks and crannies due to the fact you took such a massive tool to the rock.

I prefer to think of myself as an archeologist with a chisel and brush. Slowly, and painstakingly excavating the story.

So where to start?

Where do you get your inspiration? Music?

For me, music is a biggie. Great music I feel in my soul. It doesn't really matter what kind it is.

Bluesy, sexy music with a hint of danger and thrill to it always tells me a story. Melancholy, angry, tragic. The more emotion the more my creative spirit is stirred.

I definitely love songs that not only to the writer and singer's story but inspires me to tell my story that is simmering inside of me.

Another source of inspiration, fabulous movies energize me. They make me want to go out and create. The best movies make me fall in love with the principle actors and actresses and make it easier for me to "cast" my story.

Television dramas inspire me. Whether they be fantasies, straight ahead dramas, or police procedurals, I love them all.

Of course, there are the books. Books always have inspired me.

Then being in love can fuel that fire. Or finding your muse can sustain you for years. Daniel Craig in pretty much everything inspires me. His performances fuel my creative fire for some reason and have since I discovered him in Casino Royale.

So your hero wants something. Something seemingly insurmountable stands in his or her way.

You have your jumping off point.

You have different sources of inspiration.

You have your hero, villain and guide.

By god, you're now ready to scribble on paper or sit down before a computer.

You need a muse?

That will be discussed in the next chapter. Now go out there and start that book!

Chapter 22
Finding Your Voice, Finding Your Muse

The ironic thing is I found mine quite by accident. In the process I rediscovered my power, and found my purpose. I had two serendipitous conversations, one with my best friend and writing partner and the other with my publisher at the time. Missy Goodman and Lea Schizas.

Missy suggested I do a blog covering my life. Lea suggested I do a "blog with bipolar" writers. Wrangling myself when I have bipolar is hard enough, I told Missy no would care about my life, and rejected the notion that five writers would ever do their job without a concerted effort from me and frankly, I'm just too lazy for that. It's hard enough to wrangle myself.

Those mornings when I can't get out of bed, when I have a hot ball of emotional pain and rage, or conversely, I wake up crying, feeling lost and alone for no particular reason, it's hard enough for me to do a blog post, energy wise, but those negative feelings are what get spilled on the blog page. And weirdly people relate. They are either struggling with bipolar disorder, someone they know and love has bipolar disorder. So I found my voice quite by accident .

Initially I had a blog that was about writing, but it was the golden age of publishing, every bitch had one of those. The idea was, how did I set myself apart from that? I mean my best friend and my publisher at the time had handed me part of the puzzle. Had planted those bipolar seeds. But initially it wasn't enough to make it push up through the soil and grow.

I was writing like a mad woman. But I watered the soil with Daniel Craig movies, and the occasional book. It really did take a year of gestating. Then one day I got a wild hair up my ass and decided to write an open fan letter of gratitude to Daniel.

About halfway through it I realized I was trying to cram my life story into one letter. I realized that was humanly impossible and that I was creating myself a platform. I decided to use this blog I had created as a way to tell my memoirs. And what better way than to share my memoirs with my favorite actor.

I felt pretty safe in doing it because well, he had no social media footprint whatsoever. And I was small potatoes. His management team would know me from Adam.

In other words they would have zero interest in me. It would allow me to unlock that piece of the puzzle within myself, making me comfortable enough to tell my truth.

What I realized with that first letter, was that their must be no barriers, no filters, no muzzle put of the truth. I am exceptional at letters when telling my life story. I simply tap the vein and bleed in a stream of conscious way about my life, my ambitions, my emotions, and my bipolar disorder.

Now when I talk about your truth, I'm talking about being brutally honest. By that I been you hold nothing back.

Not in that I'm free to be an asshole way, but in that coming to terms with your own mental illnesses, issues, or trauma way.

Learning to mine that for fiction or non-fiction will be your most powerful lesson as a writer. Novel writing is about using a lie to tell an emotional truth.

My muse for the last ten or so years has been the actor Daniel Craig and everything he's been in.

In the past other inspirations and muses have included Russell Crowe and Maurice Benard, David Duchovny, Gillian Anderson, and Kate Winslet just to name a few.

Their work would fuel me. Their physicality, intellect, acting style all informing the characters that I wrote at the time. But upon seeing Casino Royale everyone faded.

The moment Daniel Craig emerged from the ocean like a gorgeous greek god, surrounded by ocean blue water and a sun shining brightly down upon him. Illuminating him like the muse of mine he was destined to be.

My imagination whistled sharply and let me know straight away, that a new sheriff was in town. I knew immediately that Daniel Craig was the muse that would ascend to the throne.

Don't get me wrong I didn't and don't know him. I'm pretty secure in saying he doesn't have a clue who I am.

I use his work to fuel my imagination. He was the hero who helped me smash through the publication glass. Once I unlocked the door as to what kind of stories I wanted to tell they started coming fast and furious. (No, I don't send any cars to outer space.)

I liked to tell action adventure and dystopian/scifi stories. I was heavily influenced in the beginning by his version of James Bond, and Cowboys and Aliens.

A novel fueled by motion picture stories and actors. I know it sounds weird, but it was a turning point for me. Casino Royale changed everything for me. It's not overstating it to say without Casino Royale this path I'm on wouldn't exist.

I cleared a path of my own.

My heroes Jane Holland, Michele Val Jean, Lea Schizas, Tony Acree, and L. Andrew Cooper, Pamela Turner, Melissa Goodman, Theresa Weston, Anabelle Munro, Lureen Wu, and Del Weston are all my loves. They have cheered me on and pushed me forward. Tim Druck, Barbara Ehrentreu, Ana Jobrail ect. John Spalding. All these people have played a role in finding my footing and finding my voice.

My filmmaker's voice is still developing.

Clint Gaige, Mark Maness, and Valyo Gennoff have all played pivotal roles. These are all the people who make up my heart.

When I created the Letters to Daniel blog it quickly became apparent, no matter how hard I would resist it, my platform was mental health and my brand was Letters to Daniel. I was branded the mental health girl.

I am first and foremost a storyteller.

I am after that, an advocate.

Those things have quickly and unapologetically become entwined. Some can't see the storyteller at times. As frustrating as it is they only see the advocate. But the truth is I'm both. There's no getting away from it.

By writing on the blog to Daniel, I found my voice. And was continuously renewed by my Muse. I encourage you all to read voraciously and view films hungrily, see what lights your creative fire, then look within and feed it.

Chapter 23
The Playlist, Music Always Sets the Mood

Music is the food of love. Love is food of creative inspiration. And elbow grease, that's the motor to make it all go.

I love to write. It's fun. It's an escape. But it reminds me that anything is possible.

You can create who worlds out of words while listening to and discovering the most gorgeous of music. I often come to the party late when it comes to musical geniuses. Mostly because I am transfixed by film scores.

I know, my love of film inspires all the things that I create. I feel I am extraordinarily fortune to be free to create and not worry if there's food in my belly, a roof over my head, or clothes on my back.

But the truth is, even if I did, I would be finding a way to do what I love. I would find a way to hear music. Music is not only a pleasurable thing, but a relaxing thing when I can't focus. It allows me to write.

Such as today.

Today I haven't been able to write much because I've been attending AFM, American Market, networking. Getting email addresses and managed to schedule two more meetings set after the conference.

There's nothing I'd like to do more now than dive back into AFM. But 5 emails and 2 meetings is a major thing. At some point tonight I will have to unwind. But I even have a pitch at midnight.

Music soothes my savage beast within.

Music inspires and lights the creative flame.

Music lets me know everything is going to be okay.

Life and writing are similar in that you get out of it what you put into each of them. Life will not always be easy. If you spend your life staring at greener pastures, or longing for what others have instead of writing and spinning your yarns about what you have, what you know and love, about stories you are bringing to the world; you will be forever unhappy. You will be forever unfulfilled.

Where is your sanctuary?

Who sings and soothes the savage beast for you?

What band lights the creative fire within and lights the way for you?

For me it depends on my frame of mind. These days it's Christmas music I want to hear. It lifts my spirits. When shopping this time of year Christmas songs are in department stores, on car radios, and I can curate songs on Amazon.

I don't write holiday stories but I will highlight the Christmas season. It can be a romantic time. It can be a lonely time. Some of the most beautiful music is the most melancholy. And that kind of music fuels the engine.

Writing stories about grief and pain and finding your way through it. Music fuels my underdog spirit. And this morning I'm happy to say I'm ready to take on the world. I haven't been much on writing the past few days but I have been trying to find the music that will unlock that drive that seems to have been waning.

This time of year is hard for me anyway.

I have bipolar disorder, the depression seems to be especially bad this time of year. And finding the music which will help me to keep scribbling words and maintain my vision is sometimes more crucial than plot, theme, or character.

Sometimes getting through a chapter bopping along to my favorite Christmas songs is enough to do what I otherwise couldn't. Curating a special playlist to distract me from my anxiety is crucial too.

Facing the infamous writer's block? For me facing a blank page can be intimidating. Writer's block is anxiety by another name for me. And for some reason music helps tremendously.

Some people say coffee makes words.

It can easily turn on you like a rattlesnake.

Just like tequila worm turning, caffeine is a lesser god that gives and takes away for me. Ask my sister about tequila, and I'll tell your stories all day about how I can go from happy writer to bitter and burnt out bipolar rage if I ingest too much of caffiene.

So, like anything in life, there's a balance to be struck.

If you figure out how to do that, let me know.

Too anxious to write, curate that list.

Too distracted, pick movie soundtracks and scores that will soothe you as opposed to agitate you.

Music can transform your writing, hell, it can transform you. And is an indespensible tool in the writer's toolbox. The list I made currently has everyone from Billie Eilish, Stephanie Ray, Dido to Hans Zimmer and Lin Manuel Miranda.

It makes me relax and propels the creative machine at the same time.

Writing a novel is no small fete. Non-fiction can be just as hard. And anything to make it easier is worth using.

Of course I have Royale Deluxe and Chris Cornell on this playlist too. So rocking and rolling to get going in storytelling fashion is another thing altogether.

I want everyone to know is music IS the food of love. It's something I can count on to soothe me when maybe I'm in a dark place, and it can coax the story out of me when I all thumbs at getting to the heart of the matter.

Chapter 24

Candles, You Inspiration Item, & the Heartbeat of Your Tale

Before I launch into a complicated lesson. I pause for the lesson before the lesson. The fact is my best writing comes from tragedy and pain and what I am dealing with right now is tragedy and pain. Grief and the time of year that just brings the struggle of chronic depression and the inability to land on solid ground.

When you're in the middle of it is the worst.

Suicidal ideation becomes a battle. The idea of closing your eyes and just not waking up becomes a thing. Where you're praying to God to please release you from the kind of pain idiots say God puts you through for a reason.

Having bipolar disorder and creating, writing, filming whatever, is tricky. People ask me if I want to be 'cured', I think they're asking the wrong question.

People like my parents, are scared by the darker shades of the disease. They think a bad day equates a need to threaten me with institutionalization. When that is actually the worst thing they can do. As Missy would say, even if you're thinking it, keep your mouth shut and think of something less triggering to say.

Navigating that while creating is the hardest thing in the world, write now I just want to beat something until my knuckles are bloody and raw and throbbing so this anger and grief will leave me.

In the last year I lost my aunts and Del to covid-19. My aunts because it was early on in the pandemic and their was no real answer to the disease. I won't go into Del's situation as it is more complicated and I blame a certain individual for bringing the disease to his doorstep while using him to further their career.

Still I lost another friend to a heart attack.

Maybe it's just all hitting me now.

This morning I'm listening to a curated playlist and writing this journal like entry because I know, even though I'm hurting and hurting badly right now, I know someone is going to benefit from knowing, when they are writing a book and they are experiencing chaotic or dramatic emotions they can survive being taken out to sea as long as they deal with the emotions head on.

It's okay to cry.

It's okay to scream.

It's okay to stumble and fall.

There's help out there. There is no shame in taking the hand outstretched. Taking the meds prescribed. Going to a therapist.

Do you have to feel the feelings? Yes. Because if you do, and you buck the stigma, and go from surviving to thriving you can have a rich, varied , and wonderful life.

I have to remember the price of love is the pain that comes when they're gone. I'm struggling with that now. But I know when I get through it, there can and will be beautiful works of art.

Usually, I light a candle. I try to make it a lavendar candle because it's a soothing aroma. As you can tell that first lesson turned into the next one. Candles just set a certain mood for me and release the anxiety that tends to get pent up in my being. For you it may be a glass of cold ice water that chills you the fuck out when sitting before a blank page.

For me it can be coffee, candied jellies, and candles. These ritualistic things help me settle in to write. The truth is I have taken to liking writing really early because everyone is in bed and if I need silence, I'll have it.

There are three other adults in the house plus a cat. I love them all. I love my cat the best of them all. But of course I love my mom, dad and aunt jan. But being alone and able to focus is pretty fucking hard. So up early I am.

What is your object of inspiration? It can be an item, a work of art, a person. Just have it on your desk.

Vision boards are extremely helpful to.

Dreams are essential. Are you dreaming of an Oscar? An Emmy? An EGOT? For me that was always a part of the dream. And while its not what drives me at my core I'd be lying if I said I didn't want it.

I think of Hamilton.

There's a million things I haven't done, but just you wait.

My desk is covered with James Bond Funk Pops, trophies repping victories, directors I idolize, and pictures of my cast and crew of Letters to Daniel and an autographed photo of Daniel himself from Skyfall.

These are inspirational items or totems.

The next thing you need is to find the through line of your story. It's pulse. It's heartbeat, in other words, what drives your tale.

What excites you about your story? What stories make you excited to sit down and pen them?

For me all kinds of of stories drive me. Look at those playlists we talked about a few chapters back. Think about what drove you into the library to checkout those books and movies and music.

For me there are two through lines. Mental health and love heals. I champion the underdog. I empower them. Those are my through lines.

What are yours?

You want to write, what's stopping you?

Chapter 25
Don't Ask For Permission

Don't ask for permission. Another of version of this might be, don't wait for the perfect time. If you have a story burning in your heart it's not only okay that you tell it, it is imperative that you do it.

Keeping things trapped inside is no fun.

But sometimes spilling our guts isn't feasible. That's when fiction comes in handy. If you're looking for permission I get it. You got bills to pay, you got mouths to feed and ain't nothing in this world for free.

We've all got the same 24 hours in a day, 7 days in a week, and we all get to choose how to spend it. You might have yourself trapped into the kind of thinking that it has to be "right" time.

Waiting for permission, or for everything to be perfect is a mistake. It will just never be the right time. Everything will never be perfect. The past and future are non-existent and can be seductive in many ways. The truth is, the past is a memory, the future is not guaranteed, all we have is now, the present.

It's hard to accept our time on this earth is finite, and we only can do so much with that time.

Having been robbed of those 14 years of adulthood being symptomatic bipolar disorder I can't stop writing. I feel like, everyday of sanity and physical health, is a tremendous gift. I don't intend on wasting it.

Granted, to me if you really want to be a published author, you'll find a way to accomplish it.

Don't wait.

To paraphrase Marisa Tomei in My Cousin Vinny, my life clock is ticking. (Cue stomping foot to wooden porch.) I lost fourteen years to this disease. And having lost 4 family members and friends to covid and other health issues, I hear second hand on the clock ticking my time on this earth.

I want that brass ring. So I'm reaching for it.

I've ridden the roller coaster of emotions in my career. Listened to the slings and arrows that impuned my talent as a writer and a filmmaker. It's hard dealing with that. Most times I could give a fuck. Every now and then it gets to me.

But truthfully so many great things are happening to me now in my career I can't complain.

Although I didn't ask for permission, it took Del Weston saying it's okay to want success. It's okay to be recognized, and by god I believed him. Having his and Theresa's wind at my back is a big part of the reason I'm at where I'm at.

I'm not *just a writer anymore.*

No one in this day and age is only a writer anymore.

Because of technology, Amazon building it's company on indie writers backs then screwing them over. Still I came up the ranks during the golden age of publishing when the world was the writers oyster so to speak.

It's not so much that way now. There are a multitude of small publishing houses, people who self publish. But the truth is New York is where the prestige is at.

I have countless books out through small presses and indie press. I have worked endlessly and with a vigor I know I had to embrace.

Building a career brick by brick, not just writing a novel. Writing the novel is the first step.

These days you need to have a handle on social media. Now, I specifically keep my political views to myself. Some make their beliefs and views a part of their brand and I suppose that's one way to do it.

I suppose I am to some degree, while wrapping my genre stories in mental health themes and wrapping my mental health themes in genre storytelling.

I didn't wait for permission and neither should you. Breakout of that shell and claim your storytelling right. I can't wait to see what you do.

Chapter 26

New York, Small Press, or Indie Press

There are many roads to take in the publishing world. Although I would say the golden age has passed that made a plethora of author superstars, well a lot of us seemed to get our fifteen minutes of fame them. Facebook hadn't revealed its true nature. Twitter wasn't overrun by political speak yet. And creating a blog about writing in and of itself was unique.

I also had a website that I kept up.

So you've written the book.

Polished it and edited it.

Now what?

Now you have some choices to make. Indie press is for me like instant gratification. I'm control freak too, and indie allows me to control everything. Of course it means all costs fall on your shoulders too. All responsibilities for getting a cover, both digital and print. Pay to have it edited. Then proper formatting of the galley.

All marketing and touring is on your shoulders too. Want it in bookstores? Look into ingram spark. Cover services? Try Fiverr. And editors, that one is going to cost you, but in the end you'll be grateful you shelled out the money.

So you don't want to be responsible for that, there are e-presses and small presses. But vet them. Some close as quickly as they go up. They generally cover the costs of the cover, editing, and formatting and publishing of the book.

No matter what well intended promises they make you, be prepared the shoulder ALL marketing and convention going costs. Only one of three of my original small press publishers remains standing.

So that's something to consider when choosing what route to take.

But finding champions for your work is essential. Creating a foundation of credits is crucial and small presses can be a very viable way to get your name and work out there.

You want to be a bestseller at least 5,000 in sales and a connection to the paper or publication whose list you want to be on.

That brings us to the Big 5 New Publishers.

That's generally what everyone thinks of when they think of publishing success.

New York.

Signings.

Paid book tours.

Uh, hold the boat.

Those book tours are your responsibility. Those signings must be arranged by you.

I should only have to write, you say. I shouldn't have to spend time marketing my work but the truth is, if no one sees your work, hears your work, no one will buy your work or publish your work. Or at risk of mixing metaphors, produce your work.

So you have to market yourself and your work. Or find someone who is willing to help you do it.

But I don't want to won't fly anymore.

Do you have a unique to you story? Create a blog share your content. A lot of people are doing Patreon, but that doesn't work for me.

I'm the queen of the blog and we'll probably start doing readings of my books. And posting them to my g1nbc blog. I'm looking email more people. Expand my backlist's availability.

There are things about marketing you just have to accept.

It has to be done.

No excuses. Don't like it? Don't care.

That's not to say I don't appreciate the introverted nature that makes us good at what we do can be a real hindrance. What I'm saying is you have to find a way to get around it.

To be clear I'm not saying, "just get over it". Social anxiety is a very real problem and can't just be healed by a wave of a magic wand. But learning how to cope and strategizing from that first point, can and will help you tremendously.

What social media do you need?

The choices are endless, so I'll give you the advice that was given to me.

Facebook/Meta.

Twitter.

Personal Website.

And blog.

I would go so far to include linkedin. Lots if unmined opportunities lie there. That's how I found my agent and manager. Find your niche. Your platform. And your brand will follow.

Chapter 27
To Agent Up or To Go It Alone

This kind of feeds into the last chapter. All I can say, many roads lead to this. And read the fine print.

I've heard it said all agents are liars. The wrong agent will lie to you all the fucking time. Sometimes the dynamic can be toxic even. Other times individuals just aren't in their right mind. Still when shopping your book around for representation.

If you are determined to go the agent route there is one of two ways to do it. Well, there's several ways to do it.

The traditional way. Write the most amazing query letter possible. Research literary agents who fit your genre. And fire emails off with the required package. It's cold querying. And it's honestly the most tedious and mind numbing thing ever. Just writing about it bores the shit out of me.

Then there's researching the conference route. Worthy conventions often have agents attend that you can pitch. Often if there's no time to pitch you can buy them a drink and get to know them and bring your project up organically. Often times if they don't rep your kind of book they will recommend someone who does and let you drop there name as a recommendation.

It must be done organically, asking for a referral at the top of your conversation is a mistake.

Don't worry if your nervous, I and plenty of authors have been where you are at this moment.

If you want to know how I did it I wrote for the small press and independently for ten years. I had as many as three small press publishers at one time. Overall I have been published 30 times and have written 34 books. 11 of them Amazon Bestsellers.

By building a portfolio, applying traditional methods, and networking and marketing across social media, I finally found an agent.

What kind of portfolio did I have?

30 published novels/memoirs.

11 Amazon bestsellers.

Several wins and top ten finishes in the Critters Preditors and Editors awards.

Several wins and finalists at Moondance and Megafest.

Write out a CV of everything you've done until now.

It will make you see all that you've accomplished up until now. Do you specialize in short stories? Think about self-publishing an anthology of your work.

I walked a ten year path to getting my agent. I really lucked out. She was working with me as my manager already. She said she would be willing to work to make it happen. She's a boutique agent. I'd rather have her because she can give me the attention I deserve and my career needs.

You want instant satisfaction? Indie publishing is the way to go.

Small presses are a great way to start building your portfolio. You get the legitimacy of being published by a name without having the output of cash up front for editing and cover art. Though you're looking at backend costs for any of these three things.

Early in on in your career you're not going to be a GOH. So you will need to have money for vendor tables. Call and arrange your signings and appearances.

This all takes time and money. I know you don't want to hear this. You need to be hustling day and night. I don't want to hear bullshit excuses. What do they sound like?

I don't have time.

Folks, we're all given the same amount of time.

I've been doing this for x years already.

Tough. Consistently working hard does ultimately yield results.

I have no money. Neither did I. I utilized free trials. Free subscriptions to software. Sometimes you just have to knuckle up and pay for stuff.

Gofundme was my best friend in my career. Networking became my super power.

So there are several paths to success. All them require getting outside your comfort zone. If you're not willing to hustle, to network, and market yourself on top writing then consider keeping writing a hobby.

Writing for me, is bliss, but a career. A career in the arts demands you work your ass of and having faith that it's all going to pay off.

I work thinking there is no endpoint. A career in the arts is about the journey. It will be hard and arduous, but the creating is what it is all about. That is where the joy and gratitude is. And if you can keep your head and heart in that you should be able to make the decision that is right for you.

If you can operate from joy and gratitude anything is possible and the marathon you are running will end in tears of joy not in tears of defeat.

Chapter 28

The Networking Game On A Zero Dollar Budget

Folks, there are many demarcations of success. I suppose it depends on what success means to you, because it can mean many things. I visit this theme often on my stories and in my non fiction work. I find success means for me, I must be constantly creating.

And who do I dream of. Well, if you've seen any of my work you know that my muse tends to be the actor Daniel Craig. I know a lot of novelists envision New York banging on their door with a six figure deal and a paid book tour. The cold hard reality that is all up to you.

Getting a publishing deal of any sort, let me say, needs to be celebrated. First of all that you finished a book at all-there's something to be said for that. A lot of people like to talk about doing it not everyone does.

Being published by a small press is nothing to sneeze at. They operate under very slim margins, you may have to be even more extraordinary to get a contract with them.

There's something to be said about being brave enough to set out as indie publishing.

The reality is I've been fortunate enough to cut my storytelling teeth in both these venues and do well in them. But, if I'm honest with myself I long for that traditional route. It's just another challenge that keeps my hunger sharp, and the fire in my belly roaring,

Another thing, it's the most recognized platform there is to want to do non-fiction work and reach the most people like me, and believe me there are a lot of us out there.

What do I mean by that?

Women, people of color (I'm white, but I am a fourth Apache), indigenous, disabled (or differently abled, however you identify yourself), and the LGBTQIA community, or any other marginalized group.

I have bipolar 1 with mixed episodes, anxiety and PTSD. I like to joke I have more letters than a PhD after my name.

Let me say, if you are able to get out of bed and brush your teeth everyday should be applauded. Sometimes getting out of bed period is the prize. Sometimes there is very real anxiety to facing the blank page.

Some keys and tips to managing that.

Grounding yourself. Place your feet on ground, close your eyes and count to fight and focusing on the present.

Deep and concentrated breathing.

Listening to music that will inspire you without interfering with your creative process and keeping those negative symptoms in check with whatever you are living with.

So for me, by following my bliss, it has led me to wanting to not only create but mentor through books and movies and podcasts. Sound impossible?

To borrow from Nike, impossible is nothing.

There are so many paths to being published now. As much as I'm looking for the next book to excavate from my soul, professionally I'm looking for the next mountain to climb. And the real joy is having your friends and family to rejoice in those accomplishments.

It's like playing a professional sport. You can have a comfortable or even flush and award winning career in the minors. There's just something about being called up to the "show".

It remains for society, the standard bearer for success. Let me rephrase that, it is the typically recognized by the lay person standard bearer for success.

The truth of the matter is no one can define success for you.

You have to define it for yourself.

My three biggest successes.

I have survived bipolar and the worst it could throw at me and lived to tell my story. Quite literally in just about every form.

I trained for and completed a marathon pre-diagnosis.

I just celebrated my ten year publication anniversary and my seven year filmmaking anniversary.

Number four on the list is somehow figuring out how to ride the waves of my illness. There are still the occasional peaks and valleys, but for now they are far outpaced by the rolling hills.

That's the greatest success. I get to do what I love. All my basic needs are met. My life is rich with my friends and family who love and support me.

I know typically I should have bought my first home by now. Owned a car. Married and had children.

I have a special needs furbaby with diabetes. You laugh but it's true. I am an award winning bestselling author, screenwriter, podcaster and filmmaker.

Letters to Daniel is the bringer of all things beautiful. Which brings me to this, Letters to Daniel started out as a blog where I could tell my memoirs. It is the place where the upward climb to success started, and cemented the fact I would become a fierce mental health advocate. But if you had told me I would be going into my sixth season of the Recovery Unplugged Podcast being in the mix at the NAACP Image Awards I would have told you for lack of a better word you were crazy. But here we are, getting ready to delve into the game of fiction podcasts. Here's how I came to be at that place.

Chapter 29
The Eternal Search For Representation

I almost forgot. At this level, no matter what industry your pursuing, your going to start inquiring do I need an agent? Where do I find one? How do I get one? Here is where I resurrect the marathon analogy.

You are not going to be plucked from obscurity. You're going to have make yourself visible to the public and research who reps what you write.

If you are going with a traditional Big 5 publisher chances are you are going to need an agent. The search for a literary agent can be as tiresome as the more isolating parts of writing a book can be.

It is a marathon unto itself. Like a race to be run within the race of getting published. You've chosen to reach for the brass ring ultimately so you have to know, it's going to take some time. Maybe your not some delayed gratification person. That's why I tell you have to find your joy in the creating. That the joy must drive you.

I've been writing since I was five or six years old and I always "knew" I wanted to be a published author.

I was introduced to the success program at that age and once a week I was given a prompt to jumpstart my stories.

I finally got really representation after ten years in the publishing game. It was something of a relief.

There's cold querying, there's attending conferences and pitching that way, there's participating in competitions.

You need to know if you're attempting fiction or non-fiction.

Know what materials the prospective agent requires and wants to see. Send them exactly that. Don't get fancy.

And finally don't nag the agency when querying them. Now I will actually move onto the next section. Getting into podcasts.

Part III
Venturing Into the Podcast Waters

Chapter 30

I'd never thought I'd do a podcast.

It's a video podcast. And sometimes during a live broadcast technology will make us its bitch. We just dipped into our sixth season and have interviewed Elizabeth Gerald, Valerie Whitcomb, Janet Kirchheimer, and Michael Caissie. All intriguing and interesting people with a lot to say. The name of my show is Recovery Unplugged and is about how one's mental impacts their professional and personal lives.

The journey from author, to screenwriter, to filmmaker, to podcaster demands that I take a bit of a detour and give someone credit for being a heavy influence on my career. And that, ladies and gentleman, is the voice of my generation, Kevin Smith.

He credits Richard Linklater.

I credit him and his titular film Clerks, with planting the seed that yes, I too could do what he was doing from my perspective and through the mental health lens.

I just watched CLERK. The documentary about him.

I've also been fortunate to see him live and in person.

As Daniel changed my life in an emotional way, it is not overstatement that Kevin was the one who put it my head and I just worked insanely hard just like him.

Now he is the King of podcasters. In a world filled with podcasters there are many imitators but few originals.

There are things about is journey that mine mirrors. My creative partner, Missy Goodman is a cross between Scott Mosier and Jason Mewes.

She was the reason I could do any of this.

Emotionally, she's my best friend and sister. But she's also a creative and deserves to have her space. Kevin is mature enough to set Scott free to be Scott. I think I'm in a weird spot where I need the stability Missy provides. According

She tends to move at her own much slower pace than I do. I would dare say I'm more driven than her at this point. That is not to say she is any less creative. I think my drive subsumed her and I have been dragging her along with me ever since we met and she suggested we partner up.

There was this part in Clerk where Kevin explains he realized he realized he had to let Scott go be Scott.

Maybe I should let Missy go be Missy. She definitely deserves that. But I also feel that fear and anxiety tugging at me. I've leaned on her for so long that I sometimes forget I was doing this stuff before we met.

And she before me.

Together we made something of a dynamic duo.

But she's like Jason Mewes in that we've lived some seriously traumatic shit together. I think I've mentioned I have bipolar disorder.

Our friendship and writing partnership survived that. We lived like hand to mouth. And survived that. She's my hetero lifemate. And now she's going to have to teach Mewes how to be Mewes.

More on that later.

After making twenty-three films with her, including the one to launch us to the next level, Letters to Daniel in all its many forms, is our "Clerks" which is opening doors previously closed. Similar themes of mental illness and mental health weave around our "Letters to Daniel" aka View Askew universe. I would "lol" here but I fear it would seem bragadocious.

So why a podcast?

And why now?

I am on my sixth season. Recovery Unplugged LIVE! And we have amazing conversations on there and I've really grown as a host.

It has made me sit down and gather up my more ambitious scripts fx and storywise. Kevin Smith is a big part of this. I know podcasts are trending, but I am not a trendy person. I'm just thinking of a unique way to get my work out there and raise awareness of my creative work.

My Recovery Unplugged LIVE! Podcast is a passion, but can be very draining. We've had heavy subjects like the holocaust and keeping the flame alive as the survivors pass on and keeping their memory alive so that maybe we can truly someday NEVER AGAIN.

I'm looking forward to fiction podcasts of my scripts. We have countless scripts. And are in the process picking the best ones to cast and record.

I don't know what will come of it. But I'd be an idiot not to.

I say all this with the caveat, this is how I've done it. There are a million ways to make it in the entertainment industry. There are steps to take that some people say I can't. It's too hard. I don't have the time. I have a family. Folks there is no such thing as "the right" or "perfect time".

I've been waiting to stage a musical version. Dude I found a collaborated and we're two songs in already. I wanted to do a one woman show about how God and Daniel Craig impacted me. The great intender, just became an awesome collaborator, you've just got to decide to take the leap and believe in yourself.

I'm not here to field why you can't. *I'm here to tell you why and how you can.*

I stared death in the face and survived. (Covid)

I got stable and have remained stable, after two breakdowns. (Bipolar Disorder)

I ran a marathon and finished it. (26.2 miles, bitches)

I endured going to bed hungry and waking up hungry every day for six months.

None of that shit stopped me and it doesn't have to stop you either.

Everyone always doubted me, except Missy. Then I hustled, directed, and as Lin Manuel-Miranda sings, I wrote my way out. You can too. Go out there and show them what you got!